# DRIVING THE BILLIONAIRE

## A SWEET ROMANTIC COMEDY

### LAURIE BAXTER

ZUZU BAILEY BOOKS

## ACKNOWLEDGMENTS

Many thanks to Chrissy Wolfe for her skilled editing. To Kate Berger for yet again being my literary test pilot. To Geralyn Corcillo for volunteering to read this and then liking it so much (especially awesome considering what a great writer *she* is). And a huge shout out to the online indie author community for always being so welcoming and supportive.

CHAPTER ONE

"The stars sure are pretty tonight," he said.

"It's like they're shining just for us," she answered, her eyes glistening.

He leaned in close, his voice low. "Maybe they are."

The picture-perfect characters on the screen grinned as they met in one final, perfect kiss. The camera tilted to reveal a glittering, star-filled sky, and the closing credits began to roll. Curled on her couch under the afghan and hugging a throw pillow, Sabrina Hopewell burst into tears.

"Oh, that's a good one! *Happily Ever Valentine*, right?" chirped her roommate, Ava, coming into the room behind her. Sabrina grabbed the remote and snapped off the TV.

"I was just flipping channels. There's nothing on." She surreptitiously swiped at her eyes as Ava opened the fridge behind her in their little kitchen. Not a lot of privacy in their tiny Queens apartment, but that was the price of being struggling theater people. Normally she didn't mind, but right now . . .

"What are you talking about?" Ava said. "It's Valentine's Day. ChikFlix is running romance movies nonstop."

"Exactly. Uck. It's complete BS."

"Girl, I thought we were past this. I know you're a secret sap. I love that about you."

Ava came around the couch and flopped down next to Sabrina. Even though she was still in her robe, her tight, black curls in a haphazard mass atop her head, no makeup on her dark skin, Ava was gorgeous. Sabrina, on the other hand, looked like one of the street kids from *Oliver!* Good thing Ava was the actress and Sabrina's aspirations were confined to the invisibility of the page.

Ava lifted her orange juice to her lips and glanced over at her roommate. She froze midsip when she saw her face. "What's wrong, Bree?"

Damn. Apparently, she hadn't hidden her little pity party as well as she'd hoped.

"Nothing."

"Were you crying at the *movie?*"

"No . . ." God, she'd make a terrible actress.

Ava squinted at her.

"You *love* that movie. It always makes you smile. You watched it at least six times last year."

Sabrina got up and busied herself in the kitchen fixing herself some toast. "It's nothing. I'm fine. And those movies are ridiculous. I'm done with them."

Ava folded her arms across her chest and stared at her.

"What? I shouldn't be watching them anyway. I need to be watching classics. Award winners. Stuff with nuanced characters and snappy repartee to help hone my writing craft, not mindless froth that'll seep into my scene construction and turn it to mush."

That sounded good, right? And it was true. She stopped, catching her breath, aware her cheeks were flushing.

Ava just shook her head. "You cannot let that weasel do this to you."

Okay, so, *yes*, her sudden emotionality and general aversion to sappy romance had a little something to do with her ex's new girlfriend moving in with him so soon. Oh, and the rock that was now on said girlfriend's finger. Which Sabrina happened to see in the elevator yesterday because, you know, of course she had been foolish enough to date a guy who lived in her building.

A Rockefeller Center proposal. While they were ice skating. In the snow. (She'd overheard them recounting the story to a neighbor. It was not a large elevator.) So romantic. Sabrina almost wished she'd thought of it herself—oh, wait, she had!

She had fantasized about it—corny as it was—and in a love-blind lapse of judgment had even *told* Brady about it, and now he was living it, except he had recast her part as a busty redhead from his gym. (Who, honestly, was likely a victim of his nonsense as much as she'd been, and Sabrina would consider warning her if she could think of any decent way to do it.)

The upshot being that clearly the universe was telling her to get her head out of the clouds and stop believing in fairy tales. For the sake of her writing *and* her heart.

"He isn't doing anything to me. I just need to do what's best for me. And chasing some romantic fantasy is not it."

Ava eyed her dubiously over the rim of her juice glass

but said nothing more. A perfect time to change the subject!

"So, do you think Ben will actually clean his apartment for your big date?"

Ava's eyes popped open. "Oh yeah, I forgot to tell you! His roommate came down with the flu, so he's sacked out on the sofa and his girlfriend's over there making chicken soup and trying to nurse him back to health. Ben and I were going to move our big cooking and candlelight thing over here. In fact, he should be here in an hour or so. I hope you don't mind. Obviously, you're more than welcome to join us."

Ava and her boyfriend—one of those too-cute-for-words, totally perfect-for-each-other, totally in-love couples—had been planning the day for a month because it was their first Valentine's together. They definitely didn't need Sabrina around, raining on their cozy date for two.

"Maybe I'll go out. You guys should have some alone time."

"Yeah, totally! You could see a show or go window shopping! I'm sure you can find something to do that would be way less boring than staying here." Ava was way too nice to say anything, but it was clear from her enthusiasm that she'd love it if Sabrina just happened to have other plans that night.

And she was right. There was a lot to do out on the town. It was New York. It was also Valentine's. There'd be flowers and music and cupids and couples in love every single place you went. And the Empire State Building all lit up in honor of the day. It was even supposed to snow later. The city would be one giant romantic cliché. Ugh. No. She couldn't. Not even for Ava. She just couldn't.

She'd just lock herself in her room all night with her laptop and a tub of popcorn. Maybe work on her short script for the upcoming showcase. Or watch YouTube videos of cat fails. If she timed her bathroom trips just right, they'd hardly know the other was there.

"Or not," said Ava quickly, studying her expression. Sabrina had never been good at hiding what she really thought. Ever. "It's totally fine. This is your apartment too."

Then she wrapped her arms around Sabrina and pulled her into a hug, and Sabrina knew she must look even worse than she felt.

Ava's phone rang. She pulled away to grab it off the counter, giving an exasperated sigh when she saw who it was.

"It's work," she told Sabrina. She shook her head and hit the talk button. "Hello?"

Annoyance flashed across her face.

"What? No. Nooo. No. I've had today off on the schedule for a *month*." Ava drove for a private car service. It was good money, but they were always switching up schedules and calling her in at the last minute. "Well, I'm sorry if everyone else took the day off too, but I have *plans* . . . I guess that's your problem, isn't it?"

She hung up, flinging the phone onto the couch.

"I can't believe them. It's Valentine's Day."

It *was* Valentine's day. And Ava and Ben had this whole plan for a romantic day together. Never mind work calling. Sabrina was going to ruin it just fine all by herself, which they definitely didn't deserve. The way she was feeling, she'd probably come out halfway through their meal and start listing divorce statistics. If only there were somewhere she could go that wouldn't make her insane.

"They actually wanted me to drive some rich dude all the way out to some tiny town way up in the corner of Connecticut. That'd take me half the day. Maybe more if that snow hits."

An idea started to form as a slow smile spread across Sabrina's face.

"Call them back," she said.

"No way, I'm not—" But Sabrina had disappeared into Ava's room.

She reemerged with Ava's chauffeur's cap jauntily on her head.

"Call them back."

oah Prince set down his overnight bag and shifted the light wool car coat he had flung over his arm to look at his watch. He didn't use the car service often—in fact, he was only doing so today because he had already given his personal driver the night off. But they had always been punctual and professional.

Though when he'd called to request the ride, he remembered now, he'd overheard they were short-staffed today. And they were only five minutes late. No, his antsiness wasn't about this slight inconvenience. It was about his irrational but real need to get the hell out of New York and fast. He sighed.

"Everything okay, sir?" asked Carlton at the concierge desk.

Noah gave him a quick smile. "Fine, thanks."

"Would you like me to take your bags, sir?"

Noah looked at the older man, then down at his own hands, small suitcase in one and briefcase in the other. He didn't get to use the private gym in the penthouse of the luxury building quite as often as he'd like, but he was pretty sure he could handle it.

He chuckled. "I'm good, thanks."

"Very well, sir."

Normally he would ask Carlton about his grandkids. Ask him if he had special plans with his wife this evening. But he was just too anxious to get out of there to carry on anything that might pass for normal conversation right now. So instead, he jiggled his leg restlessly and continued to stare out the ornate entry doors at Fifth Avenue.

In his pocket, his phone rang.

He set down his bags and pulled it out to look at the screen.

Vicky.

A twinge of guilt ran through him, but there was just no way he was ready to speak to her right now. If he had been, he wouldn't be fleeing the city now, would he?

He hit *ignore* and slid the phone back into his pocket, picking up his things once again.

Where was that car?

SABRINA ADJUSTED the chauffeur's cap in the rearview mirror as she waited for the light to change. She should have had plenty of time to get to her schmancy pickup destination after dropping Ava at home, but she couldn't figure out how to program the GPS in the top-of-the-line, next year's model luxury sedan. (She swore it was like something out of a James Bond movie.) Finally, she'd given up and just used her phone, but by then she was running late.

She didn't even know who she was picking up, just where (only the most famous and exclusive building in the city) and when (ten minutes ago). Even the end destination had only been given to her in terms of GPS coordinates. Part of the service—privacy, discretion. Whoever he was, she just hoped he was understanding. She'd had enough trouble talking Ava into letting her take her place today— that she'd agreed at all was a testament to how much she did really want to spend her day with Ben *without* a third wheel. As far as the car service knew, they had handed the key fob to their trusted employee. They had no idea said employee had turned around and handed it to a civilian (in desperate need of escape). If this guy complained, it would come back to Ava and not her.

Unless somehow he figured out that Sabrina didn't actually work for the car service. A chill ran down her spine. Ava would lose her job. They could even take legal action. Okay, no. She just couldn't let him know. She'd be the perfect driver. Attentive, deferential, whatever it took.

She pulled up in front of the main entrance to the building, a grand, elaborate affair with gilt carvings framing the imposing glass doors. Of course, it was flanked by perfect ten-foot topiaries wrapped in white twinkle lights on either side. It looked like something out of a movie. It looked like something out of *Happily Ever Valentine*.

Sabrina suppressed a feeling of nausea and panic. It was fine. She'd only have to be here a minute, then she'd be off up the FDR Drive, breathing in exhaust and speeding away from all things that screamed romance.

The door began to move, and the uniformed doorman scrambled from his station on the carpet to open it for whoever was inside. An overnight case and a well-tailored pant leg emerged first, but the midday glare made it impossible for her to see the man headed her way. Judging by the address and the glimpse she'd gotten so far, probably some stodgy old billionaire who would spend the entire trip on the phone with his stockbroker. She hoped he wasn't a cigar smoker. She still hadn't figured out how to raise the glass separator between the front and back seats.

Then he stepped out onto the sidewalk, and she recognized him instantly. Noah Prince. Aka Prince Charming. The most eligible bachelor in the city and the collective romantic fantasy of half its population. And she got to spend the next three hours playing driver to him. Because, apparently, the universe had a wicked sense of humor.

HIS DRIVER, a petite blonde about his age, was glaring at him. *Glaring* at *him*.

That was interesting. People didn't generally glare at him. People loved him. Or at least the him he had to be when he was anywhere there were people. Charming, witty, outgoing. It was exhausting.

This was new.

This woman didn't even know him. Why was she glaring at him? Maybe, he thought, suddenly feeling bad, she had been called in at the last minute when he ordered the car. And if they were short on drivers today, any new requests would require them to bring someone in who had had the day off. And it was Valentine's Day. Oof. He'd been so caught up in his own panic . . . well, he definitely didn't want to be *that* entitled jerk.

He offered an apologetic smile as she approached him.

"Sorry to have made them call you in today. I hope I didn't ruin your plans."

She looked up at him, her crystal blue eyes searching his for just a moment, and he instinctively held his breath.

"I didn't have any plans," she snapped. And with that, she snatched his bags from him and stalked off to stow them in the trunk.

He watched her diminutive figure retreat. She was all of five feet tall, her uniform blazer a size or two too large for her, her hair a mess of curls shoved under her chauffeur's hat in an apparent (failed) attempt to control it. The combination made for quite an interesting effect.

She slammed the trunk and shot him a look over the top of the car.

"Well? Ready to go?"

He suppressed a smile, the first he'd felt since everything had begun that morning.

Maybe he was partly looking for something to distract himself from his current dilemma, but this tiny, hostile driver was very interesting indeed.

He slid into the back of the car as she climbed into the driver's seat. He leaned forward, offering her a hand.

"Ms. Jenkins, I presume?" The company had given him her name when they called to confirm the reservation. He made it a point of knowing and using the name of everyone who worked for him. Valuing employees wasn't just a company gimmick—for Noah, it was a personal philosophy.

She spun around to give him—was that a *suspicious* look? He had no idea what he could possibly have done to earn this wrath, but if he needed a distraction, this was definitely fitting the bill.

She relaxed her guarded expression down to a tight smile. "You can call me Ava."

"Hello, Ava." He smiled. "It's lovely to meet you. I'm—"

"I know who you are," she said, her eyes flicking over him.

Then she whirled back forward to buckle herself in, nearly sending her hat flying in the process.

Okay, then. Frankly, he wouldn't have cared if his driver had been a newly licensed teenager who listened to death metal and spoke no English, so long as he had made it away from here. But this? This was going to make for an interesting ride.

## CHAPTER THREE

*S*abrina pulled out into the midday traffic, determined to use the rearview mirror only for driving purposes and not to examine the larger-than-fiction, perfect male specimen currently seated just a few short feet behind her. She failed miserably.

Honestly, though, what were the odds? She knew the car company Ava worked for catered to the rich and famous, but why-oh-why did today's rich-and-famous client have to be Noah Prince? Why not Paris Hilton? Alec Baldwin? Or maybe one of the Olsen Twins? Or, hell, why not *Ryder* Prince, Noah's frankly more famous (okay, notorious) older brother?

Anyone but the suave, sexy, and swooned-over younger heir to the Prince Resort Hotels dynasty. Anyone but "Prince Charming."

If this were a play she was writing . . . Well, she couldn't have thought of a worse situation to put her character in. Get your heroine up a tree. Throw rocks at her. Ideal for dramatic tension. Not so great when it's your real life.

Ugh. She stopped at a light and glanced in the mirror again. He was staring out his window, looking deep in thought. Dark, swooping hair. Lashes longer than most women she knew (and without the help of mascara). He had smiled at her before, and she swore a cartoon glint had sparked off his teeth with a *tink*. And his 10-zillion-dollar suit fit him like a glove—assuming you were wearing a glove over the body of a star athlete.

He was even more beautiful in person. Of course he was.

And . . . good Lord. Now that she looked closer, she realized he was wearing a red silk tie that matched her blouse perfectly. Like some sick twist on matching prom date ensembles. Seriously? Good God.

Just then, he looked up and caught her staring. She quickly looked away.

"You know where we're going, right, Ava? The company gave you the destination?"

"Mmm-hmm!" she squeaked.

Ava. Right. As far as he knew, she was Ava. And if he was unhappy with the service, it was Ava who'd receive the complaint. At her job that paid her well and gave her the flexible hours she needed for auditions and which she'd been nice enough to let Sabrina borrow today so she could escape.

For Ava's sake, she had to be nice to this guy. And, after all, it wasn't his fault he was an adorable billionaire taunting her new resolve to *not* think in romantic fantasy clichés. Although he really didn't have to be studying her with that vaguely amused smirk on his ridiculously handsome face right now.

It was the same look he'd had earlier when she—

Oh God. The initial shock was wearing off, and her responses to him were now playing in her head unfiltered. She'd been rude to him. Not just a little rude. Really rude. Twice.

Or rather, Ava had, as far as he was concerned. She had to make this better!

She glanced up in the mirror again, flashing him a smile.

"Anything else I can do for you today, Mr. Charming—" She winced. "Mr. *Prince*?"

He coughed and forced a smile. She needed to quit while she was behind.

But she wanted to make sure he'd give Ava a good report (or at least not a bad one). She glanced at her phone on the seat beside her. Ack! Her turn was coming up, and she needed to get over. She switched lanes, then glanced back at Charming and tried again.

"Can I get you anything? Music? An afternoon cocktail?"

What was she saying? It was barely noon, and the minibar was in the backseat with him anyway.

He opened his mouth as if to say something, then stopped, apparently thinking better of it. She was making things worse. What would an actual professional driver do?

Oh! Close the divider thingie! Yes! And that would have the added bonus of keeping her from putting her foot in her mouth anymore.

She searched around the dashboard for the button. The switch had to be there somewhere. But there were a dozen controls, none of them labeled. Who was this car made for? People too elitist to read?

She tried a button. Turned out to be the wiper fluid squirter.

She switched on the wipers and tried again. An icon lit up in front of her to let her know she had turned on her hazard lights. The guy behind her leaned on his horn. She quickly turned them off again.

She glanced up, but if Charming had noticed anything, he wasn't letting on. He seemed to be lost in thought, staring intently out the window. Scowling a little, in fact. Probably too deep in planning for his visit to a third-world orphanage or tea with the Duchess of York or whatever was on his calendar for next week to register what an underling like her was up to.

She sat up straight and cleared her throat.

"I hope you don't mind. I'd like to keep the divider open. Helps with the airflow, you know."

She gestured wildly with one arm, indicating the air. He gave her a pleasant smile.

"Oh. Sure. Fine."

Good. Okay. Good.

Maybe she could convince him she was Ava Jenkins, professional driver. Nothing to see here, folks.

Crap! Wait! Was that her turn? She'd missed her turn!

But if she just took the next right, she'd be able to double back without missing the highway entrance.

She cut across two lanes of traffic, ignoring the horns and the expletives she drew from the other drivers, and made it just in time. Now, she'd just look at her phone.

Double crap! Her phone must have gone flying when

she rounded the corner. It was now lodged between the passenger seat and the door. She stretched her arm out, trying to reach it while still navigating the side street, but there was no way she was going to get to it. She had to pull over.

In the back seat, Charming now seemed to be giving her his full attention.

She stopped the car, undid her belt, and retrieved the phone.

Her passenger leaned forward.

"I'm going to venture a guess here. This driving thing is not your regular gig, is it, Ava?"

SHE LOOKED up at Noah like a deer in headlights. A beautiful, weirdly irate, incomprehensible deer in headlights. He'd been going for light humor, but obviously, he was way too tense to pull that off. Now he'd made her nervous.

"Not *all* the time. I mean . . . some of the time. I'm fine, really. My phone just slipped, so I couldn't see the map."

"You're navigating using your phone?"

The color drained from her face, and she swallowed. "Mmm-hmm."

He really didn't care, as long as she had basic competence. He was, however, now beginning to question that. Noah didn't need trouble. He just needed someone who could get him out to the country house fast.

"You are aware the car has a state-of-the-art navigation system?"

"Mmm-hmm," she said again.

"And yet you simply prefer your phone?"

"Mmm-hmm," she squeezed.

He should have been mad or worried she wouldn't be able to get him out of midtown, much less to his destination. But something told him she was harmless.

He considered for a moment. He was about 98 percent sure she didn't know how to work anything in the car. Or navigate the city by car, for that matter. Likely she was a new hire and so had drawn the short straw for working the last-minute job on Valentine's Day.

At any rate, it was clear she didn't want to acknowledge her lack of expertise. Maybe she was worried he'd file a complaint. Some clients might have, but it wasn't his style. Frankly, he was sort of grateful for the distraction. Sure, it might be slowing them down a little, but when he thought about it, he had nowhere in particular to be today except away.

And it was even a little fun to watch her so valiantly try to prove her competence. And fail so spectacularly. There was something raw and honest about her that he found intriguing and sort of endearing.

But he couldn't let her suffer through it anymore. He offered her a lifeline.

"Okay, then, I trust you."

"You do?" Her jaw was hanging so slack he might as well have said he was giving everything up to become a mime. This woman was *not* an actress.

But, yeah, he trusted her to get him there. There was no good reason to—nothing in their interaction so far had given him reason to—but somehow, in his gut, he did anyway.

He nodded. "Sure. Hell, I don't even drive in the city. I don't have the stomach for it. Far be it from me to judge the methods of someone who does it for a living."

She studied him with uncertainty for a moment before a smile began to spread across her face.

It lit up the whole car. After the day he'd had, he didn't realize how much he needed it until it happened.

"Okay, then!" she said.

"Okay." He smiled. He couldn't help himself. Her enthusiasm was sort of infectious. And he could use all the positivity he could get right now.

She buckled herself back in and reached for her phone.

"Oh, but . . ." He couldn't help it. Whether she wanted to pretend she knew what she was doing or not, he had to tell her. "You're headed for the FDR South. That'll send us downtown, toward the Brooklyn Bridge. You want to go north, toward the RFK."

"Oh." She froze for a second, then waved a dismissive hand. "Yeah, totally, exactly." Then she feverishly punched the new information into her phone.

It was adorable. His phone vibrated with a new text coming in. Without looking, he knew it was from Vicky.

Her startled words came back to him unbidden: *Where are you going?* Called out to him as he rushed out of the restaurant that morning, having barely touched his eggs.

He wasn't even sure what he had told her. Had he told her anything or just excused himself?

His heart pounded, again.

The phone vibrated. Again.

As the car pulled away from the curb, he shifted to look out the window and ignored his phone.

CHAPTER FOUR

*S*abrina managed to steer them uneventfully onto the FDR, over the RFK Bridge, and eventually, onto the Bruckner, headed toward Connecticut. Traffic on the Hutch was lighter than she would have imagined. Maybe everyone else was already cozied up somewhere romantic with their significant others.

Though, admittedly, it was more likely the heavy, over-cast sky—threatening the promised snow but so far not producing anything—that was keeping people from venturing out. They should be okay, though. The last fore-cast Sabrina had checked had the storm delivering only a glancing blow to New York and Western Connecticut.

Her bigger problem was that now Prince Charming clearly thought she didn't know what she was doing. Maybe it shouldn't have bothered her, but it did.

She knew very well how to drive. Hell, she'd spent her formative years in a town where you practically couldn't get your mail from the box without driving. It was navi-gating the New York metro streets she wasn't so used to.

That and operating this luxury cruise ship of a car. Had there been some kind of training class? She'd have to ask Ava.

It didn't help to have a bona fide fairy-tale character staring over her shoulder, watching her every move either. If this was the universe's way of testing her resolve, well done, universe.

Okay, maybe he wasn't watching her *every* move. And he wasn't complaining either. She was grateful for that.

In fact, when she thought about it, she realized he had not only not called Ava's supervisor and demanded another driver (which he totally could have done), he had actually been pretty understanding about the whole thing. He'd actually been downright kind to her.

Which made it so much worse.

Because over-the-top charm and good looks were one thing. But kind? Kind was rare. Kind was real.

Kind was her Kryptonite.

It really wasn't fair. He didn't need to be charming and gorgeous *and* kind. Oh, and of course brilliant, at least according to the press she'd seen on him. Princeton education. Nearly single-handedly steering his father's company into a new phase of unprecedented success. Simultaneously giving back with Prince Resort Hotels' new, and of course already quite successful, charitable foundation, which he was helping build from the ground up.

Uck.

Why her? Why today?

She looked in the mirror. At the moment her passenger was riding quietly, gazing out the window. His phone had buzzed a few times with what she assumed were incoming texts, but he had ignored them. She wondered what he was doing, traveling way out to the middle of nowhere (to a location so secret it could not be named) on Valentine's Day.

For one thing, just the isolated mystery location was odd enough to pique her interest (from a purely professional standpoint, of course—her mind was always searching for interesting stories). But also, she couldn't help but wonder why he was leaving his glamorous, gorgeous, and frankly perfect socialite *girlfriend* alone on this of all days.

It wasn't like Sabrina cared about his love life. Please. She'd had enough of sappy romanticism in her *own* life, never mind caring about some overly fawned over, privileged hotel heir's exploits. But you'd have to seriously live under a rock not to know about Noah Prince and Victoria Ashby's relationship. They'd been the *it* couple for ages, it seemed, these days showing up everywhere that was anywhere together. They were a major power couple, too, running the Prince Foundation side by side and gracing the covers of everything from *Fortune* to *Cosmopolitan*. There were actual betting markets for when they'd get married and squeeze out the world's most perfect babies. Odds on nuptials before Noah turned 30 were 2 to 1. Though she wasn't sure she'd put money on that. The clock was ticking, and a full-scale society wedding took time to plan.

Okay, maybe she *had* followed this sort of thing a *little* bit in her foolish, romantic days. Which were totally behind her now.

But . . . she *was* pretty sure Valentine's Day was a

universal expectation in all long-term relationships, regardless of income or social status. So what was Mr. Prince doing out here with *Sabrina*?

She glanced back at him again.

Maybe there was a story there. Ugh. She couldn't help herself. Her writer's mind saw stories everywhere.

The trouble was, where there were stories, there were sympathetic characters. People whose circumstances had gotten the better of them. People struggling to overcome something. People you cared about, even if they were just fantasies.

Of course, maybe he wasn't the hero of this story. Maybe he was up to no good. Maybe he wasn't being *kept* from his perfect girlfriend by circumstances beyond his control . . . maybe he had *abandoned* her. Ooh! Off on some tryst! Meeting his secret lover while poor Vicky Ashby waited alone, unwittingly the victim of a scoundrel who would never come!!!

Sabrina looked in the mirror again, and the fantasy instantly evaporated. He didn't look like a scoundrel. He looked lost in thought, serious. Troubled.

Her heart squeezed.

Ugh. She hated herself sometimes.

She didn't want to care about this guy. But now, here she was, wondering what had driven him out of his normal routine. Wondering why he seemed so preoccupied. Why he was ignoring his phone. Thinking maybe he was having a bad day and—ugh, ugh, ugh—wanting to *help*.

Fine. Since her mind clearly wasn't going to shut up about this, she might as well do what she could. No harm in just reaching out for a little friendly conversation, right?

She sighed, then cleared her throat.

"So, uh, you caught me back there."

He looked up, distracted. "Hmm?"

"Before, when you said this wasn't my usual job. You caught me!" She smiled cartoonishly and made jazz hands around her face.

Prince Charming gave her a polite, reserved smile. "Did I?"

Maybe this hadn't been such a good idea. He wasn't giving off up-for-distracting-chit-chat kind of vibes. But now he was looking at her expectantly. So she forged on.

"Right. Well, of course, I do still need a regular paycheck—obviously"—she gestured around the car—"but I'm in theater. I'm a playwright."

Her lips curled at the corners as she said it. She couldn't help it. Five years after coming to the city and she still loved being able to say that. It didn't matter that she had to scrape together rent as a freelance reader/messenger/occasional office grunt. She was doing what she loved, and she was proud of it.

"Ah," he said. He went back to staring out the window.

Wow. It wasn't as if she'd expected him to get all excited about her artistic pursuits, but he could at least feign polite interest. Or maybe that was beneath his highness. Well, she'd tried. Good enough. Plenty good enough.

But then his phone buzzed again with another text, presumably, and her eyes instinctively shot to the mirror, just in time to catch his pained expression. Crud, something was wrong. Why she cared, she had no idea. But her stupid bleeding heart opened her mouth before she could stop it.

"So, do you go to the theater a lot? What sort of shows do you like? Have you seen the new Disney revival? I'm just dying to see it, not that I could score a ticket."

She threw him a grin in the rearview.

"I really wouldn't know, Miss Jenkins," he snapped. "I have more important things to worry about than the latest Broadway flop."

Ooookay, then.

Well, there you had it. Proof positive a soft, squishy heart would only ever get you into trouble. And charming princes were rarely all they were cracked up to be. Which was exactly why she had sworn off romanticism, she reminded herself.

Sabrina gripped the steering wheel harder and fixed her eyes on the road ahead. Riding the rest of the way in silence would suit her just fine.

Noah Prince could spend the remainder of this trip alone with his thoughts, however unhappy they might be.

NOAH WAS BEING A JACKASS. He knew that.

And for no good reason except that he was in a bad mood. He actually loved the theater. And despised people who treated staff poorly.

It was completely unlike him. Not that that was an excuse.

But it did tell him how much this whole . . . *situation* . . . with Vicky had rattled him.

No, he was not himself. All the more reason for him to get the hell out of the city and clear his head.

In the meantime, though, he needed to apologize to his driver. She definitely didn't deserve to have his crap day taken out on her. He cleared his throat.

"Ava, I—"

His phone rang. As in with an incoming call. He checked it, though he really hadn't needed to. It was Vicky's ring tone, of course.

Fantastic.

He caught Ava stealing a glance at him in the mirror as the phone continued to ring. If he ignored the call, it would roll over to voicemail in a moment.

Although . . . maybe if he spoke to Vicky, let her know he'd be gone for a couple of days, she'd stop calling. And stop worrying, which he knew she probably was.

He sighed. He didn't want her to worry.

"Hello there!" He cringed inwardly at the sound of his own voice. It was unnaturally bright.

When he looked up at Ava, her eyes darted away, locking on the road.

"Noah, what's going on?" Vicky asked. She indeed sounded concerned.

*Oh, I'm just having a life crisis over your suggestion and the idea that this is it for me, that's all.*

"Sorry, Vic. I suddenly remembered some out-of-town business that had completely slipped my mind." He winced at the lie, but what else could he do? "I'll be gone through the end of the week at least."

There was a long pause.

"I'm sorry for the way I ran out of breakfast. I shouldn't have done that. I was just . . . so stressed about this meeting I'd forgotten."

"Okay . . ." said Vicky on the other end of the line. Something was off, but under the circumstances, what did he expect?

He cleared his throat. "I'll be pretty swamped, so you probably won't hear from me for a while."

"This is foundation business?" she asked, a note of confusion in her voice.

Damn. Of course. He really wasn't thinking. Nice try using a business excuse when your girlfriend is also your business partner.

"No, no. For Prince Resort Hotels. For my dad."

"Oh," she said, then fell silent.

Great. For a guy known for his integrity, he was really racking up a long list of lies. But the alternative was having a conversation he was in no way ready to have.

"I'm sorry. It . . . couldn't be helped." That, at least, was painfully true.

"I understand," she said quietly, "but . . . on Valentine's Day?"

He felt guilty about that, but yes, on Valentine's Day. Because Valentine's Day was when his breakdown had come, it seemed. He realized it wasn't ideal, but frankly, if she hadn't wanted this on Valentine's Day, maybe she shouldn't have chosen today to spring her brilliant idea on him.

He pinched the bridge of his nose, squeezing his eyes shut. She hadn't done anything wrong. She hadn't even done anything unreasonable. Hell, if you had asked him if this was how he'd react to what she'd said to him this morning, he would have laughed.

Apparently, there were some things you didn't know about yourself until you were faced with them head-on.

Not that he knew jack about himself or what he wanted or *why* he had freaked out the way he had. Was still freaking out.

This was why he needed space. He needed to gather himself, to think. Then he'd come back to her a more poised, rational Noah Prince.

"I'll call you when I can, all right, Vicky?"

"Sure," she said sweetly. He could tell there was more she wanted to ask, but she didn't. Of course she didn't. She was too gracious for that.

"Okay."

"Okay."

He pressed *end* and went back to staring out the window.

SABRINA HAD TRIED NOT to eavesdrop, she really had. Regardless of her personal feelings, she didn't need to upset the client by invading his privacy, and frankly, she didn't need to expend any more mental energy on his royal heinous than she already had. But, realistically, short of sticking her fingers in her ears and singing "la, la, la" at the top of her lungs, there was no way to actually avoid hearing every word.

She felt bad she hadn't figured out the divider controls now. But she hadn't, and she could pretend she hadn't heard his conversation all she wanted, but she had, and they both knew it.

And it was pretty clear from what she'd heard that something was amiss. Trouble in paradise?

She wanted to feel snarky about it. After all, Noah Prince was hardly the sort of person who needed her sympathy. But . . . She'd heard the false cheer he'd put on to talk to his girlfriend. She'd caught his wince, making her pretty sure he'd lied to Ms. Ashby about where he was going. And something had clearly been troubling him.

The second he'd ended the call, the smile he'd pasted on his face dropped, and he just looked exhausted.

Sabrina couldn't help it. She felt bad for him. *Ugh.*

As she zipped past the Welcome to Connecticut sign, she chanced another look in the mirror. His brows were knit together, forming a worried crease between them. She felt another pang of empathy, followed by an internal eye roll as she reminded herself whatever was bothering Noah Prince was unlikely to be anything a person who lived outside of the aristocratic bubble of Fifth Avenue could possibly empathize with. Followed by an even more stark realization: that wrinkle of concern made him look even hotter.

This trip couldn't be over soon enough.

CHAPTER FIVE

*A*n hour later, they were deep into Connecticut, heading north on a smaller highway and getting closer to their destination. Flakes had begun to fall a while back, and Sabrina hadn't thought much of it, but the snow was really starting to pick up now. She would have liked to get a look at the weather map on her phone, but she'd rather not pull over, and based on their last interaction, she didn't think Prince Charming would take kindly to her asking him to check.

She glanced back at him. You'd think he would have been reading the paper or trading stock on his phone or whatever resort hotel dynasty heirs did in their downtime, but no, he had pretty much just been staring out the window since he'd gotten off the phone.

The car in front of her tapped its brakes and slipped slightly on what was presumably black ice as they went over an overpass. Sabrina's heart kicked up a few notches. It wouldn't be so bad if they had salted or sanded, but they hadn't gotten to it on this road yet. Probably because the forecast hadn't called for the storm to make it this far inland.

She wasn't a nervous driver, but if the storm had shifted, the thought of heading up into smaller back roads, where their route was taking them, then back to the city through who-knew-what was not what she'd have called appealing.

"Really coming down, huh?" she heard herself chirp.

Okay. She was a little nervous. She babbled when she was nervous.

Charming glanced up, startled, as if he'd forgotten there was even anyone else there. Maybe he had. "The help" was basically invisible to these people, weren't they?

Except. Dammit. Except there he was wearing a sort of lost look on his absurdly attractive face, plus that conversation she hadn't meant to hear but had. Yup, there it was again. Empathy. Ugh. She felt bad for this walking Chik-Flix movie cliché.

Making conversation would keep her from getting wound up about the road conditions, though, she told herself. It was true. But also maybe helped her feel less soft and ridiculous for taking pity on this guy despite who he was and how he had treated her earlier.

"If it's this bad in the city, they might even cancel the Pink Heart Ball," she offered, referencing the huge event she figured Vicky Ashby had been upset to miss. Maybe that would alleviate some of the guilt Prince seemed to be feeling.

Except instead of looking relieved, or even gazing out

at the rapidly accumulating snow, her passenger sat bolt upright, a look of alarm flashing across his too-gorgeous features.

And then a look of horror.

And *then* he actually looked like he might be sick all over the jillion-dollar leather upholstery.

"Turn the car around." His voice was low, barely audible, like he was breathing the words more than saying them.

"What?" Was her GPS wrong? Had they missed the turnoff?

"Turn the car around!"

They were on a forested stretch of divided highway, visibility not fantastic, cars cautiously maintaining speed, following in the tire tracks pressed into the snow by the cars before them. No exits in sight.

"Oh, sure, I'll just find the hover control, and then we can lift off and—"

"Turn. The car. Around. As soon as you can. We're going back to the city."

Sabrina didn't argue. He was the boss, and his tone told her he meant business. She cursed herself for having snarked back at him like that. She shouldn't have done it, but she'd already been anxious about the roads, and then he had started yelling at her.

It didn't matter. She just needed to focus on what she was doing. She gripped the wheel and kept her eyes peeled for road signs. She'd find somewhere to turn around, and they'd be on their way. Roads would be clearer farther south anyway. The larger highways heading toward New

York would be plowed first, and maybe the snow wasn't hitting quite so hard back that way. This was better, really.

"Hello?" Noah Prince sounded almost frantic in the backseat.

Sabrina opened her mouth to answer him when he continued.

"Victoria? Hello?"

Oh. He was on the phone. And he was really freaking out. Part of her wanted to know why. A *tiny* part of her wanted to offer him some reassurance or something. But most of her just wanted to get the hell out of there and back to New York already. She might have wanted an escape, but between the driving snow and the dreamboat in the backseat, she was ready to cry uncle.

NOAH HEARD a click on the other end of the line and realized Vicky's voicemail had picked up. He waited for her outgoing message to play and tried to get a hold of himself.

How could he be so stupid? *How?*

He'd realized it was Valentine's Day. Of course the heart-themed pastries at their favorite breakfast spot had made that hard to forget. He'd felt bad enough about that, but in the midst of his panic, he hadn't been able to help it. In the back of his mind, he'd known he'd need to make up for it majorly, though he hadn't gotten around to thinking about how he would do that yet. Self-preservation had trumped everything else for the time being.

But somehow, *somehow*, when he'd been busy throwing cash on the table and running out of there, it hadn't occurred to him that meant it was also the night of the *Pink Heart Ball*, one of the city's premier charity functions. It was a huge networking opportunity for New York's elite. Probably the biggest night all year for them professionally, not to mention an enormously important event for them personally, at least as long as they cared what the press was saying.

People would notice if they didn't show up to the Pink Heart Ball together. People would talk.

It was one thing for them to have personal difficulties. It was quite another to air those difficulties publicly. If he left Vicky to attend the Pink Heart Ball in his notable absence, and without so much as a well-publicized explanation ahead of time—well, what had happened between them would no longer be a private affair. It would be fodder for every gossip rag in town. Speculation would run rampant.

He scrubbed a hand over his face. No wonder Vicky had sounded not just disappointed and confused but utterly bewildered. He was such an idiot.

Finally, the phone beeped, signaling him to record a message.

"Vicky, hi, I'm so sorry. So, so, so, so sorry. I don't know how I could have forgotten. I'm in Connecticut right now, somewhere near Litchfield, I think." He looked around, but there wasn't much around them, and it was hard to read the road signs through the falling snow. "Listen, we're going to—Vicky?"

Crud. Unbelievable. He'd lost the signal. Could the snow do that? Maybe it was just a dead spot. There weren't as many cell towers up here, and a lot of the hills were basically solid rock. Get in the wrong place and all your bars would disappear.

He took a deep breath, trying to calm himself. Then he punched the seat beside him.

He dialed Vicky again.

## CHAPTER SIX

*S*abrina kept her eyes focused on the road, partly because conditions necessitated it, but also because *now* Prince Charming seemed even less happy than when he'd started barking orders.

His first call had clearly been cut off. He seemed to have been leaving a message, so he'd probably just lost the signal, though she couldn't be 100% sure he hadn't been speaking to Vicky Ashby and she'd just gotten fed up and hung up on him.

She couldn't blame the socialite if she had. Was he always like this in private? It seemed unlikely. That sort of thing was bound to leak out. Too many people around him who might be willing to sell him out for a fat paycheck from a tabloid. But if this wasn't his usual demeanor, she wondered exactly what was going on with him that had him so unhinged.

He'd been trying a second call, but after a minute, he'd slammed the phone down beside him in frustration. She glanced up. He turned restlessly to stare out the window again. She could feel the vibrations in the floor from him jiggling his leg, and his nostrils actually seemed to be flaring.

She squinted through the windshield, trying to see through the falling flakes. It seemed to be getting heavier by the minute. Great.

"I really need to get back." He said it low, maybe even to himself, but his tension was palpable and only served to make Sabrina feel more stressed than she already was.

Suddenly to her right she saw a square of bright green. An exit sign. Thank God.

She signaled, breathing a sigh of relief as she slowed onto the curve of the ramp. She would just go left, hop back onto the highway southbound, and with any luck, both visibility and cell service would be restored very soon. Then maybe her passenger would chill and she could relax as well.

Except.

The ramp spit her onto a local road, heading to the right, away from the highway, with no opportunity to turn the other way.

She glanced in her mirror, but Prince looked lost in thought, scowling out the window. Fine, at least he wasn't yelling at her. She'd just find a driveway or parking lot to turn around in and figure out where the southbound entrance was, and they'd be on their way.

His phone rang. He dove for it.

"Hi! Hi, yeah, I lost the signal. Sorry."

No way she was interrupting that. At least they had gotten out of the cellular hole they'd been in.

Anyway, she could do this, she'd just—

"Vicky?"

Oh no.

Prince muttered impatiently to himself. "Come on, come on." He was dialing her back.

Sabrina concentrated on the road. She kept following it along, though it looked like she was the first car to cut through the snow that had now covered the pavement, and she'd had to slow considerably. The road had narrowed, and the path was hilly and winding, visibility low. She could, however, see well enough to know there were no houses or businesses around. There had to be somewhere she could safely turn around. Right?

NOAH GRITTED his teeth and bit back a swear. His phone had dropped the call again.

He'd quickly punched the call back button, but of course, it didn't go through.

Son of a—

It didn't matter. He'd just keep redialing until he got through. He had to reach her.

He tried again and tried to figure out what he would say, how he would explain. But he was too frantic, too mad. At himself, at his stupid phone . . .

He tried again. And again. Nothing.

He knew they were in a spotty area, but he'd gotten the signal back once. Sooner or later it had to happen again. Except it wasn't, and he was losing what little patience he'd had.

Where were they anyway?

He looked around, suddenly realizing that the snow had gotten much worse. Branches hung low, covered in lumps of white and practically brushing the car. They were on some back road he didn't even recognize, high hills all around. No wonder he'd lost the signal.

And they were crawling along at a snail's pace. What was this woman doing? He knew she didn't know her way around Manhattan, but he wouldn't have thought she could get lost *turning around* on a major road.

"What do you think you're doing?" he demanded. "This isn't where we're supposed to be!"

YA DON'T SAY.

It took all her energy not to snap at Charming who, to be fair, seemed more panicked than angry.

But it was the last thing she needed right then. She was panicked enough all on her own. She gripped the wheel, trying to control this boat she was driving and to push aside thoughts of getting Ava in trouble, getting lost in the backwoods of Connecticut, getting buried under three feet of snow . . .

"For the love of—just turn around!"

"What do you think I'm trying to do?" she snapped. She shouldn't have, but she was pretty damn stressed, and he wasn't helping.

"I don't know, drive to Rhode Island? Turning around usually involves going the other way."

She squeezed the wheel tighter but said nothing.

"There! Turn around right there."

He indicated a spot where the shoulder got a little wider, but it was just behind a blind curve.

"No."

"No? *No*?! Yes! Just turn around! Anywhere!!"

That was it. She shot him a death glare over her shoulder.

"Listen, your highness"—flicking her gaze between him and the road—"maybe you hadn't noticed, but the driving has gotten a little treacherous here, so if you want to make it back to your downtown castle in one piece, I'm going to need you to—"

"Ava!!"

But it was too late.

THE DEER CAME out of nowhere. Sabrina had been driving country roads long enough to know to always be on the lookout, even in decent weather, but she had let herself get distracted.

She swerved to the left and managed to avoid clipping the animal as it disappeared into the surrounding trees.

Fortunately, there were no oncoming cars for her to contend with as she veered onto the wrong side of the road. Unfortunately, there was a patch of ice under the snow, which sent the enormous luxury sedan reeling across the lane.

If the car had had four-wheel drive, she probably could have brought it to a stop on the pavement. But as it was, she gripped the wheel hard and focused on slowing carefully as she steered them safely down the snow-and-leaf-covered incline at the road's edge, bumping along roughly before jerking to a stop several feet in front of a large fir there was no way around.

Her airbag popped open and then . . .

. . . all was silent.

Well, for a second. Because after that there was the sound of a seat belt being opened, then a rustling, then somehow the most handsome man she had ever seen in her life was inches from her face, looking frantic and worried.

"Ava? Ava, are you all right?" said the handsome man.

Noah Prince. Right.

The adrenaline from the last few moments had temporarily disoriented her, but as far as she could tell, she'd only been a little bounced around, not hurt. It was taking a minute, but she was starting to get her bearings. Although having Noah Prince inches from her wasn't exactly helping.

"Ava?" he said again.

Which was weird.

"Why are you calling me that?"

He paused. "Because it's your name," he said cautiously.

He was so pretty this close up. And he seemed genuinely concerned about her. It was a lovely feeling. Maybe she'd just stay here for a few more minutes.

"No, it's not," she mumbled dreamily.

The look on Noah Prince's handsome face went from concerned to seriously freaked out.

Oh, right. Oh, shit.

CHAPTER SEVEN

*I*t hadn't looked like Ava had lost consciousness when the airbag hit her, so Noah had been worried she might have been a little banged up, but not overly concerned she could be seriously injured. But now. Now she didn't even know her own name. That was bad. That was very bad.

She needed medical attention immediately, and they were in the middle of nowhere, probably not even visible from the road, even if anyone was going by. If he had been paying attention, he could have given her directions, and they wouldn't be on this tiny side road, but instead he had been so stupidly distracted by a problem of his own creation.

Not to mention he'd been berating her instead of letting her focus on the road. He'd done this. It was all his fault.

He would never forgive himself if something happened to her. He racked his brain for first aid knowledge. What were you supposed to do in the case of a head injury?

"I'm sorry." She gave him an awkward laugh. "I didn't mean that. Of course I'm Ava."

Okay, better. This was better . . . right?

But even if she knew who she was now, her momentary confusion was disconcerting. He tried to remember what he knew about concussions.

"Can you tell me where you are?"

She smirked. "No. Because you would only give me the GPS coordinates for your supersecret mansion."

He cracked a faint smile in spite of himself. At least her sarcasm had made it through unscathed.

"I'm fine, really," she assured him, patting his hand, which he only at that moment realized was wrapped across her, protectively, as he leaned over into the front from the back seat.

She seemed to become conscious of the contact at the same time because she dropped her hand abruptly.

She cleared her throat. "Are *you* okay?"

He leaned back, giving her a little space.

"Yes, thanks to you. That was impressive."

"Impressive would have been still being on the road," she said with a half smile.

She seemed to be cheerful enough, but he was still concerned.

"Does anything hurt?"

"No, I'm good. Really." She pushed the now-deflated airbag out of her way and looked around through the windows, taking in their situation. "Let's just focus on getting out of here."

The whole not knowing her name thing—even for a second—was troubling. He'd feel better if a doctor looked her over. She really shouldn't drive until she'd been checked out. He would have called 911, but a quick double-check of his phone revealed they were definitely still in a cellular dead zone.

"No signal?"

"No."

"Me neither." She sighed. "I'd like to say I thought I could back up onto the pavement, but with the snow and that incline . . ." She shook her head. "I don't think the car service company is going to be too happy if I leave their car in a ditch," she said. She sounded like she was joking, but her face in the mirror was creased with genuine worry.

"Come on," he said. Because even though he was hardly the guy you'd call to get your car out of a ditch, one thing was very clear, they needed to get out of there. For both their sakes. She needed to get checked out. He needed to get in touch with Vicky before the damage he'd already done got even worse.

SABRINA SHOOK her head and stepped on the gas one more time. Noah Prince looked so determined out there, leaning his muscular frame against the front of the beast she was driving and pushing with all his might.

But it would have taken a dozen Noah Princes to exert enough force to overcome the gravity and lack of traction that was keeping the pricey hunk of junk where it lay.

He looked like he might pull something if she let him keep this up much longer. Enough was enough. She rolled down her window.

"It's not going to budge."

"Just give me a minute," he panted. "I think it moved a little that time."

As freaked out as she was, that nearly made her laugh. The only thing that had moved was his hair, now shifted adorably out of place by a combination of the storm and his valiant, contortive efforts.

No. Not adorably. Nothing about Noah Prince was adorable.

He was a media mirage. And an ass. Definitely not adorable.

Maybe she actually did have some kind of head injury.

Why had she even humored him by letting him push at all?

He'd been so insistent, she hadn't felt like she'd had a choice.

Plus he'd been looking at her with those puppy dog eyes when he'd told her his plan. True, they were the only eyes he had. But it was still totally unfair.

The universe was clearly trying to make a point. And rub it in at that.

She opened her door.

He blinked up at her. "What are you doing?"

"I'm getting out to look, like I should have to begin with."

She stepped out into the snow and shivered, pulling the uniform blazer closed over her thin blouse. What had she been thinking when she'd told Ava to take her coat with her when she'd dropped her back home? Oh yeah, she hadn't wanted to look unprofessional with a giant puffy jacket stashed in the trunk when she went to put his luggage in. And she had *thought* she'd be inside the warm car until she picked Ava back up to return it later that night.

The worst was her feet. Her shoes—formal enough to appear professional, but comfortable for driving with just a tiny little kitten heel—were not made for a hike through the now several-inches-deep snow. Not to mention she was only wearing sheer knee-highs with them . . .

"You'll freeze." He followed after her.

"I'm fine."

She walked around the car, examining the combination of snow, leaves, and other debris the tires had half-buried themselves in as she'd spun them trying to back out.

"Get back in. We'll try again. We just need to get up a little more speed," he said. But even he was starting to sound dubious.

"Maybe if we had tire chains. Are you sure there weren't any?"

She wanted to look herself. He had checked the trunk when he got out to push, but did the wealthy elite even know what tire chains looked like?

She rounded the back of the car and saw what they were up against. The path down from the road was both steeper and longer than she had realized. There was absolutely no way they were getting out of there without a tow truck, even if there were chains hiding somewhere in the trunk. Ava was going to kill her.

All she had wanted to do was get away for a few hours. Leave Ava in peace so she didn't ruin her friend's wonderful Valentine's just because *she* was having a crappy one. She hadn't asked for a white knight to come sweep her off her feet or even for an average Joe to smile at her and make her feel remotely desirable for five seconds on an otherwise lousy day. No. All she had wanted was something to do that got her out of the apartment for a little while. And this was what she got. Stranded in the middle of nowhere with a moody and way-too-attractive billionaire, needing a tow truck she couldn't pay for and likely couldn't even call, about to get her friend fired for agreeing to this stupid plan of hers.

Happy. Freaking. Valentine's Day.

Why did the universe hate her?

It was too much. Way, way too much. So despite all her efforts not to let them, Sabrina felt the tears prick her eyes.

And, of course, that was when his royal princeliness came around the car to talk to her.

"Look, I know you're stubborn, but considering I may have given you a head injury already, you could at least take my coat. I know it's not really suited to the weather, but at least—" He stopped short when he saw her (presumably) red, blotchy face.

She swiped at her eyes, wondering if she could blame their wetness on the cold and wind.

"Hey, hey," he whispered, rushing to her side. "It's going to be okay."

So apparently, no, she could not pretend she wasn't crying.

Fantastic.

Of course it was going to be fine. She did not need his perfect face and his perfect voice and his endearingly askew hair in *her* face reassuring her. She'd rescue her own self, thank you very much.

"I know," she said tightly, afraid her voice would break if she said anything more. And then he did an unforgivable thing. He wrapped his arms around her.

"We'll figure it out," he whispered into the air just above her head as he held her close.

And he was so warm, and so sturdy, and she was having *such* a bad day, that for a moment her treacherous, treacherous body forgot she hated everything he represented and relaxed into his embrace.

He pulled her tighter. Almost like . . . he needed to hold on to her too. Which maybe he did. She didn't know what had happened with Vicky Ashby, but clearly if it had made him momentarily forget the biggest society event of the season, he must have something on his mind. Not that that excused his snapping at her earlier or his general grumpiness.

God, he smelled good, though.

This! This was the problem. If he hadn't distracted her in the first place with his I-forgot-about-the-Pink-Heart-Ball drama, not to mention his chiseled jaw and his strong arms which were now closed around her—

She pulled away sharply.

What the hell was she doing?

If sending her Noah Prince was the universe's way of testing her anti-fairy-tale resolve, she was royally screwing it up.

Well, enough of that. She'd figure out how to get them out of there and drop him at his private estate or wherever he was going and—

"You're shivering."

"What?"

"You're shivering," he said again. He looked down. "I'm sorry. I didn't mean to overstep, I just . . . You're cold. You should wait in the car, run the engine and get the heat going. I'll see if I can pick up a signal and call a tow truck."

Right. Of course. He hadn't wrapped his arms around her because he cared about her or her feelings. He just didn't want her to be cold.

Probably because her freezing to death while in his employ would play badly in the press.

"I'm fine."

"You're not dressed for this."

"Neither are you," she shot back.

He looked genuinely wounded. Maybe he really was just trying to be nice. She immediately felt bad.

Then she hated herself for feeling bad. She didn't need to go around feeling sorry for dreamy billionaires. She had enough to worry about.

He sighed and ran his hand through his hair. Sabrina ignored how this made her imagine her own fingers combing through the dark waves. Or tried to ignore it anyway.

He stood for everything she hated.

Plus he had a girlfriend.

Plus he stood for everything she hated.

"There's no point in both of us freezing," he said finally.

Which made sense. It was also chivalrous, however, and that irked her. Being close to him was doing things to her mind.

"Fine. I'll be in the car."

## CHAPTER EIGHT

*N*oah had no idea what he had done to so offend Ava, but at least she had agreed to warm up in the car.

He was glad about that. The wind was picking up, and the temperature had dropped a few more degrees. His relatively light jacket wasn't doing much to protect him from the elements. She already had a potential head injury. There was no need for her to be out there getting frostbite in that thin blouse and those ridiculous shoes of hers too.

Though he didn't have a lot of faith he was going to be able to pick up a signal out here. At least this gave him a minute to think. Unfortunately, all he could think about was how much of a mess he'd gotten himself into.

He couldn't figure Ava out either. She seemed to hate him, but at the same time, when he'd tried to comfort her, for a second there she'd seemed to sink into the moment as much as he had. Which, as nice as it had felt, wasn't helping anything. He didn't need a hug, he needed to fix this.

He needed to get them out of there, for both their sakes.

~

SHE TRIED to stay in the car. She really did.

~

"ANY LUCK?" Ava said, suddenly right beside him.

He jumped. So much for her taking his advice. Why was he even surprised?

"You scare pretty easy for a macho type, don't you?" She smirked.

He arched a brow. "You think I'm macho?"

"Nope." He couldn't decide if he wanted to strangle her or strangle her.

"What happened to warming up in the car? You've been gone two minutes."

"Two minutes are plenty." But he couldn't help but notice she had her arms wrapped tightly around herself. He was pretty sure her teeth were chattering too.

"You don't trust me, do you?"

She looked him up and down. "To fix this? No, not really."

She said it with snark, but when he looked into her eyes, he saw real fear there. Along with a heaping dose of resentment. She didn't *want* to be out here with him—she was afraid not to be.

If he was honest, he didn't really trust himself to fix this either. He had no clue how to get them out of there. Besides, there was no point in wasting time arguing with her.

"Fair enough. At least take my coat." He started to shrug out of it.

She looked at it with disdain. "No."

"No?" This woman was impossible. She was going to give herself hypothermia just to spite him. Well, forget that. He took off the coat anyway and started to hand it to her. She smacked it back against his chest.

"No. But I would like to see your phone. Gimme." She grabbed it right out of his hand. Which was not the sort of treatment Noah was used to, but that clearly didn't bother her. He stood there dumbly as she examined the screen.

She frowned. "No bars."

Which he could have told her if she had just asked. "You don't say?"

"I haven't heard any cars go by, but we haven't been here that long." She wandered away a few steps, holding his phone up in different directions, studying the display. "You obviously spend time around here occasionally. There ought to be people coming through, right? At least at rush hour."

He scratched the back of his neck and looked away. He wasn't sure exactly where they'd gotten off the main road, but the truth was it was all vacation homes up this way pretty much. Only a small population of locals. There were usually a few cars, but the storm seemed to be keeping people away. He doubted "rush hour" was going to change that.

Maybe she sensed his skepticism because she quickly added, "Or there's got to be a business somewhere along this road, right? Somewhere we could use their phone. A diner or a gas station maybe? We could just walk until we find something."

He looked over their inadequate dress. They had both planned to spend the day in a heated car. They were barely equipped to be out here for the time they had been. Plus . . .

"I don't know. Maybe, but this area is pretty rural. It could be miles." If anyone was even open. Given the way the snowfall kept thickening, he doubted that too.

No point in pointing that out, though.

He let out a frustrated puff of air. It clouded in front of him, as if he needed a reminder of just how cold it was.

"Maybe we can find some kind of magical wood sprite that will grant us three wishes," Ava said flatly.

He let out a laugh despite himself. But it faded into the muffled silence, and he quickly sobered.

He felt powerless. It was an unusual and very uncomfortable feeling for him. Not only did he feel responsible for the situation, but he was used to taking care of things. He was the guy who made everything right. Who took responsibility regardless of the situation and made things better.

But he couldn't make their current situation any better, and not only that, if he didn't, he had no hope of making the multifaceted disarray of his romantic situation any better either.

"Oh, wait, wait! I got something!" His companion squealed excitedly.

"You have a signal?" Thank God.

Her face fell. "Well, I *had* a signal. For like a millisecond."

She lowered the phone in defeat.

He stepped closer. "Let me see. Maybe I can get it back."

She'd gotten a signal once. It meant they weren't in an actual existing dead zone and the towers here hadn't been knocked out. There was a signal to be had. They just needed to find it.

She handed him his phone, and he spent the next few minutes trying every awkward arm position and posture he could think of but to no avail.

"I can't get anything."

"Let me see it again." She stretched out her hand.

"I don't think you're going to get any kind of steady connection." He sighed, handing it to her.

"I know, but when I had bars for a second, you got a notification."

His stomach twisted. Had Vicky texted him? What if they didn't find a signal and he couldn't send a reply? And what if he *could*? What the hell would he say? Or when he got back, for that matter? It wasn't like the crash had changed either what she had asked him that morning or his horrifically inept response to it.

Then it occurred to him that Ava probably shouldn't be asking to read his private texts—

"There," she said before he could say anything. She spun the phone around to him, showing him a radar map so full of bright blobs he could barely make out the New England coastline. "You had service just long enough for the weather app to update."

"Well, that's basically a blizzard."

She nodded slowly. "Mmm-hmm."

One thing he knew for sure: If they didn't get out of

there soon, they weren't getting out of there for a good, long while.

If only there was a way to get a call out, they could get someone to come help them. He didn't like the idea of Ava being stuck here without a thorough medical exam as well.

There had to be a way. He just needed to think.

The cell service in this area was notoriously spotty. There were too many rocky hills around. They blocked the path from the towers, and the only way to get a signal was to get to somewhere . . .

He looked around them. They had spun out into an area nestled low on uneven ground. Just beyond the row of trees, there was a rise covered by a fairly steep outcropping of rocks. It was probably what was shielding them from the nearest tower.

And if he could get to the top of it— "I think I know how to get a call out."

"Oh, really? Do you have access to some kind of secret rich person 5G I'm not privy to?"

He bit back a smile. This woman did not let up.

"Something like that. You go wait in the car this time, okay? For real? I've got this."

"Oh, sure," she started, her tone just as sarcastic as before, "I'll just . . ."

She stopped when she followed his line of sight to the top of the rocky peak.

"Oooooh. Okay then. Let's do it."

And then she ran ahead. Of course she did.

## CHAPTER NINE

"I still think you should stay in the car," he said in his stupid handsome voice as he caught up to her. "There's no point in both of us having to climb up there."

Sabrina wasn't sure how a *voice* could be handsome, but somehow he managed it.

Regardless, she wasn't about to let herself be rescued by a *Prince*, thank you very much.

"Fine." She stopped and turned to him with a smirk. "You go wait in the car. Warm up."

He sighed. "At least let me find something heavier for you to wear in my suitcase."

Of course. No way a nice boy of his breeding was going to let a lady do something like this on her own. Well, that and she suspected he had only agreed to let her come because he was still worried about her after the accident. He probably thought he was covering it well, but she had caught him studying her with concern several times since.

Which made sense, considering he thought she hadn't

even remembered her own name. It was almost funny, but he had looked so sick about it she almost wanted to tell him the truth to put him out of his misery. She was worried about Ava's job, but honestly, her intuition told her he wasn't going to rat her out.

Except, she reminded herself, she had sworn off listening to her intuition along with all other dreamy, romantic notions. Her gut wasn't to be trusted, and neither were random eligible billionaires. Let him worry. He'd get over it.

As for his offer of something warmer to wear . . .

She looked at the rocky hill ahead of them, not so much a long climb as it was a steep one. Basically a small cliff. And it looked like the wind was harsher at the top, where there were hardly any trees. Okay, fine, her chauffeuse ensemble was starting to feel a little thin. Like nonexistent thin.

"If it'll make you feel better." She shrugged.

She trekked back around to the back of the car and popped the trunk. He opened his bag, digging inside for a second before producing a thick (and admittedly tantalizingly snug-looking) wool sweater. She pulled it over her head and pushed her arms through the sleeves.

It was like a dress on her. She shoved the cuffs back until her fingers poked out but kept the rest of her hands covered.

She closed her eyes and sighed.

Okay, yes, it was bliss not to be freezing anymore. And she was just going to ignore how delicious this sweater smelled. Like aftershave and laundry detergent and man. She was probably just delirious from the warmth anyway.

Because no actual human male had any right to smell that good.

"Better?" he asked.

Her eyes flew open. "Yeah. Sure. Let's get going."

All right, maybe she had forgotten he was standing there. She blamed the sweater.

He looked down at her shoes. "I wish I had something you could wear on your feet."

Yep, next time she stole a driving job from Ava, she was definitely packing some hiking boots. And a coat. And a satellite phone.

"Eh, I'll be fine." She waved him off. Truthfully, she was probably in danger of frostbite if she stayed out too long in these, but she wasn't going to admit that to him. She marched on, leaving him standing alone by the open trunk.

"All right, all right," he called after her. "Wait for me."

Sabrina stifled a squeal as her foot slipped. She recovered her balance and glanced behind her. Her companion hadn't seemed to notice. She'd have to watch her step—never mind the cold, these shoes had zero traction. But she wasn't about to advertise that to him and have him go all he-man on her again and try to leave her in the car.

"Come on," she called over her shoulder, "time's a-wasting!"

THEY WERE HALFWAY to the top, though there was still no signal. Noah wasn't surprised, even if he had hoped they wouldn't have to climb all the way up to get one.

He led the way. At least he had convinced her to let him

do that. She hadn't wanted him to, of course. She was infuriatingly stubborn.

But she had ultimately conceded the wisdom of her walking in his tracks rather than sinking her basically bare ankles into six inches of snow. His dress shoes weren't great for this, but at least he was wearing real *socks*, for God's sake.

They were going slower than he would have alone—he didn't want her to lose her footing in those shoes, and he kept glancing back to check on her, worried she'd get dizzy after the head injury she was pretending didn't happen. Even so, they were making decent progress.

But it was so quiet out there. The silence was getting to him.

"So," he called out, squinting into the falling flakes, "You a city girl originally?"

She scoffed. "You're a city boy, that much I know."

Well, yeah. Everyone knew that. Everyone knew everything about him.

Or more accurately, they thought they did. "The city's not my favorite place, though."

"No? Then what is?" He heard her puffing from the effort and slowed his pace a bit.

"We were headed there," he said wryly.

"Ah, the country manse."

He choked on a laugh. He shook his head.

"It's not a 'manse,'" he said, navigating over an icy tangle of vines that ran between the trees.

He turned back to her and offered her his hand. She stared at it suspiciously for a second before sighing and taking it. He helped her over the vines, landing her beside him on the other side in the small space between low-hanging tree branches. She looked up at him.

"Thanks," she breathed.

"Sure." He was momentarily distracted by her eyes, which sparkled back at him with sapphire intensity.

She was squeezed practically up against him, and just for an instant, the frigid air seemed to still.

"Um . . ." she said.

Right.

He stepped back, giving her room. He turned and continued up the hill, but he was preoccupied.

There'd been a flicker there. There was no denying it. She was obviously an attractive woman. It wasn't like he didn't notice attractive women. He was a normal hetero-sexual guy. He was also a busy guy, with too many respon-sibilities to count. And a guy who'd had the same woman on his arm for years. So he noticed attractive women, sure. But so what? They didn't factor into his life.

It was just how it was for him. And this was no differ-ent. So why did it seem different?

Maybe, he realized with chagrin, because before today he hadn't considered whether this, his current existence, was how it would be for him . . . forever. Was he okay with that?

Did it matter?

"So what is it then?" Her voice intruded on his thoughts.

"What?" he half snapped.

"Our supersecret destination," she continued. "What is it if it's not a manse?"

"Oh. It's . . ." Normally he didn't tell people about the

house. What did it matter if he told her? She'd see it anyway . . . or would have, at least, had they not taken this unplanned detour. "It's just a small cabin. It's been in my family for years. From . . . you know, before."

"Before what?"

Before his dad had become the resort hotel king? Before their private lives had become fodder for public consumption? Before Noah's personal decisions had all become business decisions?

"Just before. When I was a kid."

The press loved to make a big deal about how his dad had built Prince Resort Hotels from nothing, like it was some kind of fairy tale. As if that was that and now they were all living happily ever after.

They left out the part about the blood, sweat, and tears that had gone into it. That still went into it, increasingly on Noah's part—even in his capacity at the foundation, and certainly in his role as heir to the dynasty itself—as they worked to keep what they'd built growing. To keep their reputation strong, their positive and distinguished image unblemished.

Especially given his brother, Ryder, who'd chosen the part of incorrigible bad boy, leaving it to Noah to be the Boy Scout. And whaddaya know? The media loved it. Which meant Dad loved it and Noah was stuck. Sometimes it was exhausting.

It was why he *needed* places like the house. Somewhere to retreat to. Something just for him. Now more than ever, as he was starting to realize so little else in his life would be.

"When you say small cabin," Ava began with amusement, breaking into his thoughts again, "do you mean only ten bedrooms and eight baths?"

He chuckled.

"Two and one."

She stopped short. "Really?" she asked. She sounded shocked.

It really was a pretty bare-bones place. He was surprised his parents hadn't tried to sell it long ago. Maybe they'd forgotten they even owned it. Not that it mattered. He would have bought it from them himself if need be.

He himself only made it out a few times a year, but . . . "It's my escape," he confessed.

She laughed. He could practically hear her rolling her eyes. "What do you need an escape from?"

He clenched his jaw and moved forward, ignoring her. She hurried behind him.

"Your private jet? Your penthouse apartment?" Her voice was playful, teasing, but it irked him. She thought she knew him. She didn't know him. He wasn't sure anyone really knew him anymore.

"Your summers on the Riviera? Your Ferrari!"

He kept walking.

"Your season-ticket box seats for any team you want? Oh, I know! Your cover-girl-gorgeous socialite girlfriend?"

That did it. He whirled around.

"Actually, yes."

She blinked up at him, all shock and doe eyes. Whoops. He was not supposed to have said that.

"Whoa, what'd she do?"

"I don't want to talk about it."

He also *shouldn't* talk about it, but either way, that didn't seem to matter to her. She hurried up alongside him, not letting it go. And why would she? It was seriously juicy inside information. Though, to be fair, she seemed as concerned as she did fascinated.

"It must have been bad. Did she cheat on you?"

Of course she hadn't, she was sweet and loyal and maybe the kindest person he knew. Which just made him feel worse.

"No."

Ava cautiously cocked a brow. "Did you cheat on her?"

"No!"

He might have royally screwed things up today, but he would *never* do that . . . and not just because his dad would never forgive him the bad press.

"Did she . . . kidnap your dog and sell it on the black market and replace it with a half-cocked lookalike thinking you would never notice and now you've been banned from the AKC?"

He stared at her for a moment, then sighed. "She sat me down for a lovely breakfast and rather reasonably suggested that we take our relationship into the logical next phase and get married."

The teasing smile faded from Ava's lips.

"Okay . . ." she began hesitantly. "And what did you say?"

"I ran out, fled the city with a flimsy excuse, and accidentally made us miss the most important social and business event of the season."

## CHAPTER TEN

*S*abrina had no clue what to say. What he'd just admitted there . . . that was kind of huge. And not at all what she expected.

He was here because he'd run away from a marriage proposal?

Judging from his rueful tone, he wasn't feeling too great about any of it either. He turned and kicked at an overgrown thicket with his fancy, expensive shoe, even though it wasn't in their way, before starting up the last part of the incline.

Victoria Ashby had proposed marriage, and he'd made an excuse and run away.

That was interesting. It was just objectively interesting.

She hurried after him, turning over this new revelation in her mind.

The crown prince of New York society was not, as he was intended to be, at a super swanky gala event with his magazine-cover-perfect *fiancée*. He was hiking in the woods with her.

Okay, that last part wasn't really his choice, but still. Still.

"So, why'd you do it?" she asked.

"I'm sorry?"

"Why'd you run? You know, from your . . . fairy-tale ending, I guess." She couldn't quite keep the hint of sarcasm out of her voice.

He let out a sort of half snort and said nothing.

They climbed a few more minutes in silence, scaling a particularly steep stretch, slippery with snow, before finally reaching the unobstructed top of the hill. The ground was rocky and uneven. They paused as they both caught their breath. The cold air stung her lungs.

"Not a believer in love?" she asked. She didn't know why she was pressing the issue. Maybe she was looking for some kind of kinship or solidarity. Somehow it seemed as if she might feel better knowing someone as swooned over as Noah Prince actually *agreed* with her that romance was all smoke and mirrors.

"Not at all. If anything, I guess I'm sort of a hopeless romantic." Sabrina's stomach twisted. That hadn't been what she'd expected to hear. He cleared his throat. "But I don't think some great romance is in the cards for me."

Suddenly, and okay, sure, probably irrationally, she was *pissed*. This clown had a perfect life. No great romance in the cards? Please. He had no idea.

"Oh, yeah, poor you. I've been following your love life"—involuntarily, of course, but it was virtually impossible not to—"Yeah, you've had a terrible time. Society events, glamorous international travel, and everything from red carpets to White House dinners, all with a woman on your arm who could be a supermodel but *chooses* to champion charities instead. No romance for you."

His face became pained. "Look, it's complicated. Those things might seem romantic, but they're more of an obligation than anything else."

"Right. So Victoria Ashby is an obligation?"

He was quiet, kicking the snow with his shoe for a moment. Then he looked up. "I don't know. Maybe."

His warm brown eyes stared earnestly into hers. Sabrina's heart skipped two or three beats. But she steadied herself. She knew her instincts were terrible. They were what had gotten her into trouble with Brady and every guy who came before him, frankly. She wasn't going to let them get the better of her now. She'd done enough of that for a lifetime, thank you very much.

She stared back at him for a good, long moment. A little too long, really.

"So you believe in happily ever after, but you're going to settle for 'you do what you have to'?"

Why was she trying to talk *him* into believing in romance when she had just sworn it off herself? What was she trying to prove?

He shrugged.

"I'm 'Prince Charming,' everything I do has to fit the part. Everything has to be for the good of the kingdom."

He stood there. Gorgeous, perfect, and . . . lost. His eyes looked so sad, she could no longer hold his gaze.

Her eyes ticked down to his chin, where she noticed a small cut. He must have nicked himself shaving. Such a normal, human, imperfect thing to do. And a chunk of his hair was sticking up at a funny angle again. And now that she looked at his nose closely, she realized it wasn't totally symmetrical. Just like any other person. Not perfect at all.

Not perfect. Real.

That was so much worse.

"So you'll be going back to your princess then, I assume." She was surprised at how bitter she sounded.

He breathed out a cloud of air, his jaw tight. "I don't know. Maybe," he said again.

They fell silent. She wanted to say something else, but she was stuck between "Good, it's where you belong" and "Don't bother, romance is nothing more than a sales pitch" and—worst by far—"Forget her, fall for me!" So she didn't say a thing.

Why were they even talking about this? What did she care about his love life? She barely cared about her own. She was going to focus on her writing. And he was going to do whatever resort hotel billionaires do.

They did not need to be discussing their views on romance.

It was confusing. It was messing with her stupid, easily bewitched, bothered, and bewildered brain. *Fall for me?* What was that?

Clearly Noah's presence and this heightened situation —them being stranded on the side of the road—not to mention him confiding in her about his love life, was messing with her head. Objectively interesting or not, her feelings on the whole situation were starting to feel decidedly not objective.

She was going to have to have a word or two with her psyche when she got home.

Apparently, he didn't want to continue talking about it any more than she did because after a moment, he pulled his phone from his pocket and glanced down. "I still don't have a signal. Do you?"

She checked. She did not.

She looked around them. From this high vantage point (which turned out to only be a couple hundred feet up, even though it had taken them a good half hour of careful climbing), she could see that the landscape stretched on for miles all around. There was hardly a road to interrupt it and no houses or buildings as far as the eye could see. Nothing but silence and snow surrounded them, and darkness would be coming in a couple of hours, maybe less.

She looked back at her companion, all handsome and forlorn.

Never mind the car company, or Ava, or even Noah Prince's debatable romantic woes. They were going to be stuck here—very possibly overnight, through the storm—if something didn't change soon. A prospect that made her more than a little uneasy for more than one reason.

But especially because she wasn't sure she could keep herself convinced she wasn't attracted to Noah that long.

That was when she heard it. She didn't hesitate.

"AVA! AVA, WHAT ARE YOU DOING?" Noah ran to catch up. But she was racing down the rocky incline at record speed.

He slowed to shimmy under a low-hanging branch, and that's when he saw it, barely visible in the thick eddies of falling flakes—an orange blur that could only be a snow-plow, rumbling down the road in their direction.

"Over here! We need help!" Ava yelled somewhere in front of him. He located her by the sound of her voice, a tiny blur herself, dark against the white of the snow. She was close to the bottom of the hill, but she'd be hard-pressed to make it before the plow passed them by. And their car, he was now quite certain, wouldn't be visible from the roadway.

She must have had the same thought because she raced frantically down the rocks.

"Wait!" she screamed, but it turned into a strangled cry.

Noah watched in horror as Ava slipped the rest of the way down the hill, landing in a heap at the bottom, still a good twenty yards from the pavement. Up on the road, the plow blew by, throwing a heavy wave of snow down the little drop and into the ditch where the car sat, landing with a dull thud against the metal of the trunk. The truck ground its way along the road, leaving them behind, unnoticed.

"Ava!" Noah cried out. "Ava, just stay there!"

He scrambled down the rest of the way to her, but of course she didn't wait. She tried to stand, squealed in pain, and immediately sat back down.

"Are you okay?" The words came out unexpectedly panicked. But if she was hurt, it wasn't enough to draw her attention from the disappearing truck.

"I can't believe I missed him," she said when he got to her. She looked up at him. "But he'll be back, right? Now that they have plows out, they'll be coming through regularly."

Except the area was known for its less-than-predictable services.

"It could be a while."

"Like an hour?"

"Or, you know . . . overnight."

Ava went pale. "What?"

"Yeah," he said, scrubbing his face. There wasn't much way around it. The storm was picking up. From the little he'd seen from that weather app update, except for maybe a pocket or two of respite, they could expect the snow to continue for much of the night.

And there hadn't been a signal at the peak of the hill. He suspected the closest cell tower might have been taken out by the storm after all. The snow was so thick you could hardly see more than a few yards in front of you. No one who didn't have to was going to be out in this. Another plow *might* pass, but . . . well, there was every chance it wouldn't too. In the past, he'd seen the area stick to plowing the main roads mostly and waiting for the snow to stop accumulating before handling the smaller routes, like this one.

Flakes were collecting in Ava's eyelashes as she sat there. The wind stung his face. He squinted to look at her.

"Someone will be by, by morning, I'm sure. But for now, I think the best we can do is get out of the cold. Come on," he said, holding out his hand, "let me help you back to the car."

She paused a moment, then sighed, rolling her eyes. She took his hand, and he pulled her to her feet. But when she set her weight on her right leg, she winced in pain and lost her balance.

She fell firmly against him. Noah reflexively wrapped his arms around her. She gazed up at him. Again. He'd be lying if he said he didn't like the feeling a little.

Their breath came out in visible puffs and mixed together.

"You okay?" he asked quietly.

She blinked at him. Her eyes widened. She shook her head.

"No. Yes."

She pushed away, putting a few inches between them.

"I can't stay here with you," she said. "There has to be a way. I have to get out of here."

She was so horrified at the prospect he let out a laugh. "I promise, I'm not that awful."

She eyed him a moment before cracking a tiny smile. "Says you."

It wasn't much, but just that microscopic bit of warmth and humor provided a desperately needed break from the tension of the whole disastrous situation.

But then Ava shook her head and looked away.

"No. Wait . . . What about the car? The company will be mad, they'll—" She cut herself off, freezing as if a realization had just hit her. "I don't even know if the insurance will cover me."

Now she looked really worried.

"Of course it will," he said. He knew the company. They were highly professional. They would have all the proper insurance in place. But she was genuinely frightened.

She started tearing up. "I'm not so sure. I'm . . . a very recent hire. I don't think all my paperwork is in . . ." Her breath turned jagged, and she wobbled on her good leg.

Noah reached out and held her arm, steadying her.

"Then I'll cover it!" He said it without even thinking.

She stared at him like he was insane. But if he needed to, he would pay to fix the car. Hell, he'd pay for a new one if necessary. The money was nothing to him. He just couldn't stand to see her so upset. She'd been through enough already (in no small part thanks to him). She didn't need to worry about this.

"I'll call them as soon as we get back and explain the whole thing," he added.

"No! No!" she said suddenly. He felt his eyebrows shoot up, and she added, "I mean, it's fine. It'll be fine. Let's just get back to the car, like you said."

She turned and took one big step away from him and promptly collapsed into the snow.

## CHAPTER ELEVEN

"*T*his really isn't necessary," Sabrina said, trying to keep as much physical distance as possible between them.

It wasn't easy, considering he was carrying her.

"If you squirmed less, we'd be there sooner," he said. His breath tickled her ear. There was no escape.

If she hadn't wanted him to rescue her with the car company—who would certainly have something to say about the car not being returned until the next day, even if she did manage to hide the whole tow-truck thing—she certainly didn't want him literally sweeping her off her feet. All because of the tiny detail that she didn't seem to be able to put any weight on her right ankle.

He was breathing hard from the effort of ferrying her over the slippery and uneven ground between where she had fallen and the car. And the way he was holding her meant her face naturally rested between his neck and his shoulder, her cheek up against a thin patch of skin between his collar and his hairline.

He was warm and solid, and she could feel his heart beating against her. And, she reminded herself, he was Noah Freaking Prince, icon of male perfection.

This really was cruel and unusual punishment.

They reached the car, and he managed to get the rear door open.

"You'll be more comfortable back here, where you can stretch out."

He bent to lower her inside, taking care to set her gently on the bench seat. Which, unfortunately, meant he was now pressed up pretty tightly against her.

Sabrina held her breath. She was *not* attracted to this guy.

Or rather she was—of course she was, that was basically his whole purpose in existence, being the textbook example of every woman's fantasy man. But that did not mean she had to give in to that.

She *wouldn't* give in to that.

She didn't know if she was being tested or taunted or both, but either way, she had been jerked around by fantasies and fairy tales long enough.

It would help if he wasn't quite so close, though.

"Sorry, I . . ." He glanced over her shoulder, and she realized his arm was now trapped behind her.

"Oh, right." She flushed, leaning forward immediately to set him free. He straightened up.

"You okay?"

"Yeah . . . Thanks."

And then they were just sort of staring at each other. It should have been awkward, but instead, it was oddly intimate.

He looked away—thank God—eyeing the car's trunk. "Maybe I should check for flares. Just in case someone does pass by."

She had already checked when he was getting the sweater out of his bag. There hadn't been much of anything back there, and definitely not flares (which she'd like to have a carefully chosen word or two with the car company about, thank you very much). But right now she was happy to have an excuse to get some more space between them. The proximity or the drama of the situation or *something* about all of this was clearly messing with her mind.

"Yeah, you should definitely do that."

He nodded and headed back to the trunk. Sabrina breathed a sigh of relief.

Though it was short-lived because as soon as he was gone, she suddenly became much more aware of the frigid temperature, the still-driving snow, her throbbing ankle, and the general seriousness of their predicament. Whether someone came by in five minutes or five hours (or longer . . . ), they needed some way to alert them.

She moved to slide her shoes off—even if he insisted she raise her feet, there was no point in ruining the leather with dirty, melted snow—only to discover the heel on her right shoe was no longer securely attached. Evidently her unsteadiness after her fall hadn't completely been due to her injury. Small comfort. This day just got better and better.

Noah reappeared in the doorway. "No flares."

And better. "Great."

"Maybe we could turn on the car lights," he suggested.

"I'm not sure how visible they'd be from the road." She sighed. "Besides, we don't want to run the battery down."

He nodded. "Right, but if we keep the motor running, the battery will keep its charge. We want to do that anyway, right? To stay warm?"

He offered her a faint smile.

She looked down at her lap. "If we might be here all night, we're going to need to conserve fuel."

They could probably run the engine on and off enough to keep the temperature to a bearable cold-but-not-liter-ally-freezing inside the car, but the thing had already guzzled half their gas in the slow traffic on the highway, and she was pretty sure the rest wouldn't last half the night if they didn't ration.

"Oh," he said. Now he looked down, studying his hands. Suddenly, he looked up again. "Are you sure? Because—"

"Yeah." She didn't let him finish. "I might not be quite up to speed on all the features of this beast, but I do know how to read a fuel gauge."

"Right. Of course."

"But you're right," she said finally, "If we're going to camp out down in this ditch, we need some way to alert anyone who comes by. We need something that will stand out and catch their attention."

"Agreed." He rubbed his chin. And in an effort not to stare at his exquisite jawline, Sabrina dropped her eyes.

To his shiny, bright, silk tie.

And before she could think, she reached out and grabbed onto it.

"Something like a big, *red* flag."

He glanced down. "Yes! Yes! Perfect!"

He loosened the tie, sliding it excitedly from his collar. Sabrina swallowed hard.

There was nothing sexy about this man removing his tie to use it as a makeshift emergency flag, she reminded herself. Too bad her body wasn't buying it.

He flashed a smile. "I'll just go tie it around a branch! Brilliant idea!"

His expression fell a little as he studied the tie. "I do wish there was more fabric here, though. It's a little small to guarantee it's seen. I could check my suitcase again, but I don't think—"

He stopped short. He was now staring at her neck.

Her hand went up reflexively, and she felt her silky collar peeking out from under his bulky sweater. Right. She was wearing her red blouse.

He swallowed. "I, um . . ."

Was she actually going to do this? If she had any hope of being rescued from an evening alone with Noah Prince (and all the other troubles the accident had caused), yes. Yes, she was.

She sighed.

"Turn around."

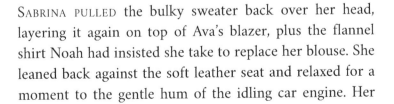

SABRINA PULLED the bulky sweater back over her head, layering it again on top of Ava's blazer, plus the flannel shirt Noah had insisted she take to replace her blouse. She leaned back against the soft leather seat and relaxed for a moment to the gentle hum of the idling car engine. Her companion had also insisted on that.

The car had warmed up nicely (the heated seats didn't hurt). This would all be nice and cozy were she not stranded here with less and less chance of rescue before morning as the snow piled up and the sun sank lower in the sky.

She shifted slightly, trying to catch a glimpse of Noah out on the roadside. He had left to secure their makeshift emergency flags where they would have the best chance of being seen. From her low vantage point, she could just see his feet, now apparently pacing the road, probably hoping against hope that someone would just happen by while he was up there.

It really was incredible, everything that had happened. The sort of story that strained belief, but with just enough bad luck for the heroine to make it suck you in anyway.

She couldn't have written it better herself.

First her attempt to flee romance lands her on the road with Prince Charming of all people for the better part of the day . . . and now she was likely stuck with him for the better part of the night. There they'd be, all alone, him taking care of her and her poor, injured ankle. It was a perfect setup for romance. Somehow he'd produce a lovely dinner of caviar and champagne (probably in the mini fridge she'd noticed built into the seat in front of her), and there'd be music and—somehow—candles. And she'd look into his eyes, and he'd look into hers and say—

"Uuuugh!!!" she screamed. Why? Why were these thoughts creeping into her head? She didn't want them there. She was done with fantasy. And she *definitely* didn't want to be fantasizing about the most unreal, perfect embodiment of—

"Are you okay?" Noah had flung open the door and was standing in the opening, pink-faced and breathless, staring at her with alarm.

"What?" She blinked at him.

"Is it your ankle?"

"What?" Normally she was a great deal quicker than this. But he had caught her off guard. There should really be a rule against sneaking up on someone who is fantasizing about you. Not that she'd been fantasizing about him.

Not on purpose anyway.

"You screamed," he said.

"I don't think I really screamed."

"You did. I thought maybe you'd tried to get up and—"

"Nope. See? Still right here."

"Are you sure—"

"All good."

"Because it sounded—"

"I'm fine. Really. Totally fine."

She locked her eyes on his and willed him not to push it.

He relaxed against the doorframe and ran a hand through his gorgeous thick locks as he let out a sigh.

"Thank God. I was so worried when I heard you. It's bad enough I've dragged you out here and managed to get us stranded in this storm. I couldn't live with myself if I thought you were just lying here in agony."

She was about to make a crack when she stopped. She could see in his face he was utterly sincere.

He was worried about her. He'd come running —*running*—when he'd thought she'd cried out in pain. And now that she thought about it, he'd done the same when she'd fallen too. Sabrina's heart twisted and melted and pinched all at the same time.

Oh, she was in agony all right, but it had nothing to do with her ankle.

"I'm fine," she said again. "I'm good. It's nothing." Because his feeling bad was suddenly somehow making her feel terrible.

"Maybe I should have a look. Just in case."

She arched a brow. "What are you, a doctor now too?"

He slid in beside her, gingerly lifting her injured leg into his lap. Which absolutely did not cause Sabrina heart palpitations. Definitely not.

"No," he said, running his hand gently along the bruise she hadn't noticed before. "But I've seen my share of skiing mishaps and such. Does it hurt when I touch here?"

Did it? She hadn't noticed. Mmmm . . .

Okay, no. No, this was not happening. She yanked her leg away.

"No! I mean, it's fine. It doesn't hurt too much."

He eyed her, looking for a minute like he might press the issue. But then he just said, "Hang on, I've got something that may help keep you a little more comfortable, at least."

He slid out the door, slamming it shut and leaving her alone. With her thoughts.

She refused to acknowledge any of them.

A moment later, he reappeared, holding a pair of thick slipper socks. He slid in beside her, pulling the door shut behind him this time.

Sabrina was suddenly aware of how small the space was

they now shared. Huge, as cars went. Tiny if you were hoping to avoid the personification of everything . . . well, that you were hoping to avoid.

"Give me your feet," Noah said, gesturing for her to put them in his lap again.

"Thanks, I can handle it." No way was she letting him put his hands on her again.

He looked dubious but handed the cushy socks over. "Sure."

She slid her good foot into the first one, no problem. And she had to admit, its coziness did not go unappreciated. But when she tried to get the other foot into its mate—

"Ow!"

There was just no easy way for her to pull the sock up over the injury herself without twisting or bumping in such a way as to cause pain.

Noah raised his eyebrows to her in question.

She let out an exasperated sigh. "Fine."

She leaned back and allowed him to finesse the thick knit over her ankle. She was sure she had merely sprained it, but it was pretty damn swollen.

A laugh bubbled up as she thought of her situation. Stretched out in the backseat with a smoking hot billionaire, her ankle the size of a watermelon draped in his lap.

Super sexy.

She suppressed a laugh and came this close to snorting in the process. Instead, it probably looked more like a strangled hiccup.

Also sexy. Good thing the last thing she cared about right now was being sexy. Also the last thing he cared about (her being sexy) since he had a hot, glamorous girl-friend. Or, actually, maybe he didn't, considering what he'd said earlier.

Not that she cared!

God, what was wrong with her?

"What?" said Noah, a half-uncertain, half-amused smile playing across his lips.

"What what?"

"Why were you laughing?"

"I'm laughing?"

"Well, you were. Then you got all flushed."

Oh, fantastic. Sabrina felt herself blush even more.

Noah looked alarmed. He put a hand on her forehead.

"Are you feeling all right? I think I read somewhere head injuries can sometimes seem okay at first, but then . . ."

She was never going to forgive herself for forgetting what her name was supposed to be and convincing him she had some kind of traumatic brain injury. The poor guy looked so worried.

She laid a hand over his. "I'm fine. Really. Nothing to worry about. Well, above the knee, anyway."

He gave her a faint smile but looked away, gazing out the window at the vast expanse of white that was practically enveloping them.

"Hey," she heard her own voice say gently. "It wasn't your fault, you know."

And for a second, she wasn't sure what he was thinking because he looked at her with such a mixture of guilt and confusion and helplessness, she had to fight the urge to fling her arms around him right then and there.

"The accident, I mean. It wasn't your fault," she said.

He searched her eyes, and for a moment all was silence and snow and the two of them and nothing else.

Then Sabrina looked down at her hand, still clasped over his, her leg still draped in his lap. And he looked down. And then they both pulled apart as fast as they could.

"I, um, I think I'll go check in the back, see if I've got anything else useful in my bags."

She nodded enthusiastically. "Yes, yes! Good idea! I'll, uh, see if I can find anything good in the minibar."

"Right. Good. Yes, because we need to eat. So . . . good plan."

"Okay."

"Okay."

And with that, mercifully, he swung the door open, hopped out, and shut it tight again, leaving Sabrina alone again. For a minute.

God, she hoped there was alcohol in that minibar.

## CHAPTER TWELVE

*N*oah rifled through his suitcase, trying to
ignore what had just happened.

Because nothing had happened.

Maybe he'd had a moment there with Ava. But surely
that was just some misguided mix of concern for her well-
being and confusion over his situation with Victoria. It
didn't mean anything. It couldn't mean anything.

Sure, there was something appealing about Ava. Her
snark? Her seeming lack of a need to feel deferent to him
as, frankly, most people he encountered did? The fact that
he'd already made an idiot of himself in front of her—
something he generally did not allow himself to do with
anyone—and she was still there?

Of course she was still there. She couldn't go anywhere.

He was being ridiculous.

Although. There had been that moment. He was fairly
certain he hadn't imagined that.

The whole situation—everything from his reaction to
Victoria's staid and practical proposition to him stuck in

this crazy storm with a virtual stranger who wasn't afraid to throw insults at him—it was all so messy and disorganized and out of control.

And yet. In its own way, it was . . . exhilarating.

It was real.

It was more real than his carefully thought out, carefully executed day-to-day life was by a factor of ten.

And even though he was freezing and tired and still worried about Ava, despite her insistence she was "fine" . . . if he was entirely honest with himself? He kind of liked it.

He kind of liked it a lot.

He couldn't like it. He couldn't do messy and out of control. He had responsibilities. People depended on him. And they depended on him to be Noah Prince.

Right. So. Back to the task at hand.

He continued to dig through his bag, pulling out the few various items he thought might help. There wasn't much. Besides the sweater and slipper socks he had already given Ava, there was another pair of thick socks and his flannel pajamas.

He had traveled light since he kept quite a few things at the house for any winter visits he might make. Unless his aftershave could be used to help them weather the night, that was about all he could manage.

Even if they could only run the car intermittently, as long as they could stay reasonably layered, they ought to be okay. An image of himself wearing his pj's with his suit flashed through his mind, and he chuckled. Under normal circumstances, he might be embarrassed to look so silly in front of anyone. Somehow the idea didn't bother him so much with Ava.

Oh, she'd make a comment about it for sure. Was it wrong that he was kind of looking forward to it?

He glanced over at his briefcase and paused. There was one more thing he had that they could use. Should he? What the hell. Desperate times called for desperate measures.

THE DOOR OPENED, sending a blast of frigid air in before Noah climbed in and slammed it shut again. His cheeks were red from the cold, and his hair was covered in a heavy sprinkling of snowflakes.

Sabrina had to fight the urge to reach over and brush them off.

He had a small pile of things he'd gathered from the trunk with him, more clothes, it looked like. She hoped he'd fared better than her.

"Please tell me this stuff is more tasty and filling than I'm imagining, because this is apparently our dinner." She wrinkled her nose as she held up the small tin.

She'd thought her idea of champagne and caviar was a joke. Turned out the joke was on her because that was literally all there was in the minibar.

"I wouldn't know. I'm not a fan myself, but I *do* have something that might help the situation."

He reached into the stack on his lap and produced a large bag of . . .

"Cheese Doobers?!"

He grinned. "Yes."

She grabbed them out of his hand. Which she probably

shouldn't have done, but the second she'd seen them, she'd started salivating, and she had suddenly realized just how hungry she was.

"Sorry. Can I . . ."

"Please."

She tore open the package and grabbed a few of the delicious orange blobs, stuffing them into her mouth before holding the bag out to Noah.

He took some, eating a lot more daintily than she was, but whatever.

"Mmm, artificial cheese never tasted so good. Where did you find these?" She paused, suddenly panicked, and began looking over the bag. "Wait, how long do you think they've been back there? What were they, wedged behind the wheel well? What if they're expired? Expired artificial cheese can't be good for you."

He chuckled. "Relax. I didn't find them, I brought them. I keep a secret stash in my briefcase."

Sabrina stared at him. He reached into the bag and popped another blob into his mouth.

"Let me get this straight. Noah Prince is 'not a fan' of caviar, but he—secretly—likes Cheese Doobers?"

"Kind of an addict, really." He licked the orange powder from his fingertips, which was, frankly, distracting.

Sabrina looked down at her lap and realized it was coated in a light dusting of orange. She looked back at him. Clean as a whistle.

"How did you do that?"

He waggled his brows at her. "Lots of practice. More?"

He held the bag out to her. She eyed him cautiously before reaching in for another blob.

"This doesn't exactly fit your public persona, you know."

"Yeah, well." He carefully removed another Doober and placed it in his mouth. "That's the brand."

Interesting.

"I do, however," he continued, "enjoy a good bottle of champagne. Shall we?"

He nodded in the direction of the minibar.

"Sure."

Why not? It was either that or eat the snow.

"I THINK that's enough Cheese Doobers for me for now," Ava said with a groan. "Although they do go surprisingly well with champagne."

"See, I told you."

Noah sealed up the rest of the bag and set it on the ledge behind them, beside their champagne flutes. The snow had completely coated the rear window and covered most of the car. Maybe that was why he hadn't noticed until now that it had gotten dark outside.

In addition to polishing off half his contraband snacks, they had donned the rest of his warm clothes. He now wore his black watch plaid pajama top under his suit and car coat. Ava looked rather adorable with the matching bottoms pulled up over her slacks. But it was still cold.

They had shut the heat off a little while ago to save fuel. She slid her hands into his extra socks, which he'd insisted she take as makeshift mittens, but he noticed she was shivering.

"Why don't we turn the heat on again for a bit?"

She paused, probably calculating how much fuel they could afford to burn. He was definitely going to trust her on that. Somewhat embarrassingly, he really did have no clue when it came to cars.

"Okay, yeah," she said finally.

He leaned forward into the front and pushed the start button.

"Nice, but you have to go put your foot on the brake, remember?"

"Right." Definitely embarrassing. He hopped outside, slipping quickly into the front. This time he successfully started the car.

Ava laughed as he returned to his seat.

"Been a while since you've been behind the wheel yourself, eh, Billionaire Boy?"

"Something like that." He smiled despite himself. No one had ever called him Billionaire Boy before, that was for sure. He doubted anyone else would dare. Maybe that was why he kind of liked it.

A silence fell over the car. They'd set out their flags. They'd eaten. They'd bundled up. There wasn't much else to do but wait.

He turned to her. "How's your ankle?"

"It's okay, thanks. I think the champagne took the edge off a little bit. Kinda pricey for a painkiller, though." She gave him a little smile.

They settled back again, both staring ahead.

"Oh, wait!" He remembered one control he *had* seen on this car. He leaned into the front seat, found the button he was looking for, and—

"Ooooh!" she gasped.

A thousand LED lights lit up to create a mock night sky on the car's ceiling.

He leaned back, and they both gazed up for a few minutes without speaking. Finally, Ava said, "The stars sure are pretty tonight."

"Yeah." Then he added, without really thinking, "It's like they're shining just for us."

Ava practically choked. "I'm sorry, did you just quote *Happily Ever Valentine* to me?"

He could feel the color rising up his neck, but he smiled sheepishly. "I told you I was a bit of a romantic. You like that one too?"

"I used to." She looked away for a moment before turning to him more brightly. "Anyway, what now?"

"I don't know. That was my big trick." He gestured to the lights. "That's all I've got."

She shifted in her seat and raised a brow. "Really? The great Noah Prince, and that's all he's got?"

"Don't tell anyone."

"I'm just keeping all your secrets today," she pointed out, but she grinned as she said it. "We could play a game."

"Oh, sure, I'll just go grab my chess set. Oh, wait . . ."

"Ha, ha. We don't need a chess set. We could play something like . . . Two Truths and a Lie!"

"How does one play that?"

Ava's mouth dropped open. "Oh, come on. You have to have played this game. You went to college, right?"

He nodded. "Princeton."

She rolled her eyes. An amusing if unusual response. "Right, of course. Then you must have played it at some point. It's one of those classic college games, you know, usually played among many friends and even more drinks."

"Ah, well, that explains it. I didn't do much socializing in school."

She just stared at him. Her eyes sparkled in the dark. "Well, now I just don't believe that."

"It's true. I started working for Prince Resort Hotels the summer before my freshman year. I spent half my time in college working to keep myself at the top of my class and the other half commuting to the city to learn how to run the company. Not much time for drinking games."

"Really?"

He gave her a little shrug.

"That's terrible."

"Not so bad. I did end up with a multibillion-dollar company I get to help run, so there's that." He laughed here, mostly to convince her it was fine, since she looked genuinely sorry for him.

That was a first. He wasn't used to people feeling sorry for him. It made his heart squeeze in a funny way.

Truth was, as excited as he'd been to get in and start working his way up through the executive track, he had felt like he was missing out, watching all his classmates cut loose . . . have fun . . . date . . .

"Do you want to know how to play?" she asked, arching a lovely brow. Spending the evening cooped up in a luxury sedan making up for lost silliness in his youth with this woman? There were worse things he could be doing.

"Please."

## CHAPTER THIRTEEN

"My name is Noah, I like Cheese Doobers, and I am sixty-two years old."

He smiled at her. Sabrina groaned. She had hoped the game would give her an opportunity to learn more about Noah Prince—from a purely writerly standpoint. She had realized she was unlikely to have this sort of opportunity again, and she had realized that no matter how much his over-the-top idealness disgusted her, a young, handsome billionaire was, objectively, an interesting character.

Perhaps she might use him as the victim in a murder mystery, for instance.

But first she had to get him to understand the game.

"Right, yes, but you have to make them all things I don't already know about you. So I have to try to guess which one is the lie."

"Ah." He knit his brow. "Maybe you could show me. Why don't you try?"

She eyed him suspiciously.

"I'm stuck in a storm. I have blonde hair. And I'm

beginning to think you're playing dumb to get me to talk about myself."

Why he would be interested in her she couldn't imagine. Maybe he was just trying to avoid sharing anything too personal. Yeah, that made more sense.

He feigned deep thought for a moment. "Hmm. None of those things is a lie."

He grinned, and holy crap, her heart did this crazy flutter thing. This was something she had not known about Noah Prince before today—his smooth, buttoned-up public charm had nothing on his playful teasing.

It was killing her.

He had to be deflecting in order to preserve his privacy. The teasing was just part of the distraction . . . although . . . that theory didn't mesh with the secrets—big and small—he had already disclosed to her.

"Come on, Ava. I'll play if you will."

That shook her back to reality. Right. Ava.

So she had a choice here. Whose truths was she going to tell? She looked up into his eyes, warm and brown and oddly sincere. And against her better judgment, she decided. She'd be herself.

Except for the name, of course. He could still turn her in to the car service management—although her gut told her he wouldn't.

But it was her one protective shield, the thing that was grounding her, reminding her that this wasn't her actual life. That none of this was real.

She looked up at the magical stars hanging above them in their cozy little campground in the middle of nowhere. And at the gorgeous man sitting across from her. So familiar from magazines and TV, but different now, with little details like the silliness of his pajama top under his designer suit and the five-o'clock scruff covering his jawline, so close she could just reach out and touch it.

She'd be lying if she said she didn't want to. But he was a mirage. A mirage with a shiny, sparkly girlfriend who would never in a million years be sitting here playing Two Truths and a Lie with the screwed up, struggling, lovelorn likes of her if it weren't for this storm.

And fate, said a stupid voice in the back of her head.

And that was exactly why she needed a protective shield.

"Okay. My name is *Ava*. I'm from Vermont, and—"

"I thought you said they had to be things I didn't know. I already know your name."

She shrugged. "You're new at this. I'm trying to go easy on you."

THEY'D BEEN PLAYING for a while, and so far he had learned Ava grew up in rural New England, double majored in theater and English at the University of Vermont, liked licorice, hated hot weather, and preferred dogs to cats unless they were yappy dogs, and then she didn't prefer either.

Moreover, he had revealed a number of small secrets that could be nonetheless scandalous if they got into the hands of the world's gossip columnists. Like his personal preference for camping over staying at his own luxury hotels. Or the fact that he had resorted to converting a room in his penthouse to a gym, complete with treadmill, because even though he loved running in the park, he couldn't take the attention he got whenever he ventured out in public these days. Or how hard he'd fought not to be named New York's sexiest billionaire by *NY Society Magazine* this year so he wouldn't have to deal with quite so many adoring fans on said runs (he had ultimately agreed when the editor pointed out how good the press would be for the business).

He really shouldn't have been sharing these things with anyone. His public image was carefully cultivated for a reason. Everything he did he did with the company's image in mind.

But, frankly, he was enjoying this. Letting her in on his little secrets—admissions he'd never make in public. He hadn't realized until he started how good it would feel to let someone see even just a glimpse of the real him. Or maybe it wasn't about letting *someone* see those snippets. Maybe this was more specific to her.

He wondered for a moment what it would be like to let her see more than a glimpse. To let her all the way in.

But, of course, he couldn't do that. Still, playing at it like this, with a woman—he suddenly realized—he probably wouldn't see again after this tiny interlude was over . . . This was kind of fantastic, actually.

There was something about her, something so raw and so real. He implicitly trusted her. He felt like he could relax and let his guard down for the first time, well, in years.

She, on the other hand, hadn't given him much. She was guarded, it seemed. Maybe she had a secret. More likely, based on her reactions to him from the start, she just didn't trust him.

That thought hurt more than it ought to have, given the very shallow and very temporary nature of their significance in one another's lives.

While he certainly didn't want to make her uncomfortable, he also felt a pressing need to make it clear he came in peace. And, for reasons he didn't quite understand himself, he wanted to know more about her. Maybe because her life seemed so different from his own.

"Tell me more about the plays you write," he said.

She looked up at him in surprise, then looked down again quickly. It was hard to tell in the low light of the car's interior, but she looked like she might be blushing.

"No, uh, you don't want to hear about that. Besides, we're playing a game."

He ducked his head to catch her lowered eyes.

"I do," he assured her. But she still looked uncertain. Maybe because he'd been so rude when she'd tried to discuss the theater and her work on the drive. "I'm sorry if I made you feel otherwise. My behavior earlier was inexcusable."

She studied him carefully for a moment, then nodded quietly.

"Make it part of the game, then," he added. "Two Truths and a Lie, theater edition."

She chuckled and drew a deep breath.

"Are you really interested?"

"I promise. I love the theater. I even know someone who's a Broadway producer."

She laughed again, shaking her head. "Of course you do."

She gazed up at the ceiling stars, and he worried he had blown it, that she would never really feel comfortable talking about anything personal with him. But then a grin spread across her face . . .

"Okay, got it."

. . . she wanted to share this—with him. A warmth spread through his chest that had nothing to do with the heat blowing through the car vents.

Ava ticked off her "facts" on her fingers.

"I wrote my first play at the age of ten, I once named a character after my childhood dog, and I once came this close"—she held her thumb and index finger millimeters apart—"To having a show produced off-off-Broadway."

She grinned at him triumphantly, eyes sparkling.

"You're supposed to guess which one is the lie, remember?"

She poked him with her toe.

Right. How he was supposed to think with her smiling at him like that he didn't know.

No, wait. He did know. He was just passing the time with a new . . . friend. He was not supposed to be distracted by things like smiles. Or toe pokes.

He shook his head, clearing it.

"Sorry. All right. I'm going to go with the character name being the lie, because you already told me your childhood dog's name was Sparkles."

Ava clapped her hands together gleefully. "Ha! *One* of my childhood dogs was named Sparkles. The other one was named Max."

"All right, that's simply not fair." He grinned.

"There are no rules about fairness in Two Truths and a Lie."

"Except the one about coming clean in the end."

"Right, yes, of course that one," she conceded.

"Okay, then," he said, playfully arching a brow, "fess up. What are you lying to me about, Ava?"

Up until then they'd been smiling and laughing together, but now Ava's face fell. She looked suddenly serious.

He reached out and touched her arm.

"Hey, I'm sorry. You don't have to tell me if you don't want to."

"No, it's fine." A smile slowly began to creep across her face again. "I actually wrote my first play when I was five."

"Really? I'm very impressed."

"You shouldn't be," she said wryly.

"So what was this debut masterpiece about?"

"Oh, it was an epic adventure about a girl who scales the kitchen cabinets in search of secret cookies."

Noah grinned. "I love it!"

"That's nothing, you should have seen my unicorn riding trilogy from fourth grade . . ."

He laughed. "That might be difficult to stage."

"I didn't have the best grasp of set design limitations back then."

Whatever had been bothering her before was clearly gone. She simply lit up talking about her writing.

It was intoxicating. He felt honored to be shown this side of her.

"And your more recent work?" he asked.

"Oh, well, they've mostly been rom-coms."

"That sounds fun!" He smiled, but she looked less than enthusiastic.

"Yeah, I'm thinking of shifting to something else. I don't need to be responsible for perpetuating a bunch of unrealistic ideas about love."

Oh. The statement was somehow disappointing. Deflating. Sure, it had been pretty clear she tended toward the cynical. But he felt sure she wouldn't have spent time writing something she didn't really love. To turn her back on that . . .

"Is that what you think you've been doing?"

She shrugged.

And suddenly it seemed very important to him that she *not* think that.

"I mean, it's romance and it's comedy, right? Love and laughter. I can't think of two more important things to bring to people. And I'd venture a guess, having known you these, what?"—he checked his watch—"six hours, that you're pretty damn good at it too."

She cracked a wide smile. "Oh, you can tell that, can you?"

He nodded. "I'm sure of it."

She studied him for a moment. He braced himself for the sarcastic insult that was sure to come.

"So my last play was based on this relationship I was in at the time . . ."

∾

Sabrina didn't know why she was telling him all this, but suddenly it was pouring out of her.

How hard she had fallen for Brady, how she'd let herself get swept up even when, in retrospect, there had been signs those intense feelings were not mutual. How she'd poured her soul out on the page, letting her daydreams run wild. How he'd broken her heart. How she now saw that she'd been more in love with the fiction of him she'd created in her mind than the real Brady. How she couldn't stand to open the script anymore.

She hadn't even told Ava how much it had affected her, but somehow Billionaire Boy seemed safe to confide in.

Probably because she'd never see him again after this. Or because her insignificant little heartbreak wouldn't register a blip in the glamorous and important life of someone like him.

Or because somehow, in this short and strange time he'd spent alone with her, and despite her newfound resolve, he'd managed to earn her trust.

No, definitely not that one, because that one was insane.

He looked at her with earnest eyes, their warm brown shining in the darkness. "I'm sorry. That must have been really hard for you."

Sabrina felt herself tear up.

"Mmm-hmm" was all she managed before the floodgates opened. He scooted over—carefully avoiding her hurt leg—and pulled her into an embrace. She leaned into him and just let herself cry. Okay, maybe she trusted him a little.

After a minute, she pulled away, pulling the socks off

her hands to swipe at her eyes with her still-slightly-cheesy fingers.

"Hey," Noah said softly, producing an actual handkerchief from his suit pocket and proceeding to wipe her tears away with it. Because, of course, he did.

Quiet settled around them as they sat there together in the glow of the fake stars. Neither of them moved away.

Sabrina gave a little shrug.

"Love sucks, right?" She sniffed. "Well, at least for most of us regular folks."

Noah got a funny look, and she worried she had insulted him (which was strange, because she hadn't been all that concerned about that earlier).

"I'm sorry. I shouldn't have said—"

He held up a hand. "No. It's not that. It's just . . ." He drew a long breath. "I don't think I've ever actually been in love."

Sabrina blinked.

"How is that even possible? You're—"

"Prince Charming. I know. But see, that image takes a lot to maintain. Not to mention the job part of my job. It doesn't leave a lot of room for—"

"No, but—" Sabrina looked down to discover she had placed her hand on his chest to stop him. What was she going to say?

That he was so much more than that silly persona? That he was funny, and kind, and kind of a dork, and that the real him was so much better than any glossy media image. That she liked him just the way he was? That he was pushing her resolve not to get swept up to the absolute limit because the way he was looking at her right now, the only thing she could think about was leaning forward across the inches that separated them and—

Noah caught her hand, which was apparently still pressed against his very well-defined chest, and held it in his.

He locked his eyes on hers, almost like . . .

Was it possible? Could he be feeling this too? Because if he was, then what would that mean for all her no-more-sappy-romanticism resolutions and even the whole idea that romance like that didn't exist?

If he was feeling it too, it would negate her whole thesis, wouldn't it? Render it meaningless and free her up for what she was sure would be the most epic kiss she could ever—

The car engine abruptly cut out, plunging them into fake-starlit silence and making Sabrina acutely aware of the ragged sound of her own breathing.

## CHAPTER FOURTEEN

"*I* think it stalled," she said. Which, duh, but she had to say *something* to fill the silence left by the absence of the motor hum and the wake of whatever the hell had just taken over her brain.

What was *wrong* with her?

Noah blinked. "Right. I'll just go—I mean, one of us should see about the—and obviously you can't really"—he gestured to her elevated ankle—"So I'll just go. Restart it."

He swung the door open and hopped out, reappearing in the front seat a second later.

Great. He was acting weird. Which could mean she wasn't the only one this was awkward for.

Could he tell what she'd been thinking?

Oh, please God, no—she would be mortified.

Because she'd been thinking about kissing him. And not in some kind of dreamy fantasy way. Nope. Sabrina was pretty sure she had been *this* close to actually throwing herself at Noah Prince.

She was an idiot.

More than an idiot.

She was an utter moron who'd done exactly what she'd set out *not* to.

This. This swoony, starry-eyed crap. This was exactly why she'd sworn off all things romance in the first place. She needed to stick with that. To protect herself—both from heartbreak *and* from looking like a complete fool. If it wasn't already too late for that.

If Noah Prince didn't already think she was another drooling fangirl, ready to hang on his every word.

Oh. Except Noah Prince had just said something she hadn't heard, she realized. Whoops.

"Sorry, what?"

"It's not starting. Maybe I should go look under the hood."

"Oh, yeah, that's a good idea."

He found the switch and turned off the interior lights— smartly thinking to save the battery while the car was off— before stepping out into the cold.

See? Right. *He* was trying to make sure they survived the night. Which was exactly what she should be doing. Not diving headfirst into make-out fantasies. Because the car not starting was actually a big deal. She needed to focus. God.

At least he didn't seem to be acting weird anymore. Maybe she had imagined it. Just like everything else she'd been imagining.

She really wanted to smack herself in the head right now, but she refrained. Idiot.

She had actually thought for a minute there that *he* might have been thinking about kissing *her* back there too.

Maybe this crazy day was getting to her. It had to be, because she was really losing it if she imagined the most eligible bachelor in the Northern Hemisphere—issues with his girlfriend notwithstanding—was just sitting here in the middle of nowhere thinking about kissing *her*.

HE HAD ALMOST KISSED HER.

What was he thinking? Maybe he hadn't made a move, but he'd been thinking about it. If the car hadn't stalled right then and distracted them...

Noah paced around the car, letting the frigid air slap some sense into him. He had wanted to kiss her.

He paused in front of the grill, realizing that he was feeling quite a bit of heat rising off the front of the car. More than he thought he should, though maybe it just felt that way because the air temperature had dropped so much. Maybe it was nothing. Still, he'd better get a look inside.

He felt around, looking for a latch to open the hood. Maybe there was a release under the dashboard that he'd missed.

Besides, what he was feeling had to be just some kind of stress response. He had just met this woman. This wasn't real.

He pulled his phone from his pocket and turned on the flashlight. Smoke or—no, steam—was billowing up from the car. Still... this was not good.

Noah tipped his head skyward and let out a deep breath.

Real or not, he would have kissed her if the car hadn't stalled.

Right. The car. He needed to focus on the car. If he could just get the stupid hood open. He shined the light along the front edge of the hood, looking for the latch.

Not to mention, she basically worked for him. *And* he had a girlfriend. Or he had this morning anyway.

He was a mess.

Finding nothing where he'd looked, he angled the light lower.

And that's when he saw it—the enormous pool of blue in the snow beneath the car.

Oh, crap.

"HOW MUCH ANTIFREEZE?" Sabrina asked, already dreading the answer.

"I mean, hard to say, but roughly? All of it."

"We must have run over something that damaged the coolant line when we went off the road." It would have been easy enough for a jagged rock to hide under the snow and leaves. It wouldn't take much for a slow leak—and it must have been slow or the engine would have cut out sooner. "Cars like this were not made for off-roading."

Noah cracked a smile and rubbed the back of his neck. "No, they were not."

The automatic cut-off valve would be kicking in to keep the engine from overheating. Which is why he hadn't been able to start it again. Which meant . . .

"So. No more heat, I guess," Noah said, reading her thoughts.

She nodded. "At least until the car cools down." Which would take some time.

"Right."

And even then, though Sabrina assumed the safety systems on the beast would protect it, she didn't exactly want to tempt fate. She was in enough trouble getting stranded overnight in the thing and now *damaging* it. It was probably a simple repair—she could imagine what had happened—she'd probably knocked a hose loose or put a small hole in a pipe . . . but that hardly mattered.

She wasn't even supposed to be there.

She was going to end up messing everything up for Ava, who had only been trying to help poor pathetic Sabrina. If she risked it, just for a few minutes of warmth before it overheated all over again? If she ran the thing on no coolant, trusting the safeties to kick in soon enough? Nope. She had no interest in gambling that the engine wouldn't seize. She'd be erring on the side of caution, thank you very much.

"Honestly, it's probably best to leave the car off. I don't want to risk damaging it. More."

"Sure, whatever you think. Your car, your call." He flashed a smile.

Heh. Yeah, her car.

A car, it occurred to her, that was going to get pretty damn cold overnight. In addition to the general awkwardness that was already hanging in the air. She shifted uncomfortably.

"So. You don't have anything else warm back in that suitcase, do you? Blanket? Parka?"

"Just some boxer briefs." It was pretty dark with all the car lights off and just the glow of the few far-off street-lights along the road reflected in the snow, but Sabrina could practically *feel* him blushing after he said it. He cleared his throat. "I keep clothes at the house, so I didn't need much. Plus . . . I hadn't really planned to take the trip. I packed in a bit of a hurry."

And on that note . . .

An awkward silence overtook the car. Not just because of the underwear, although *thanks very much for that mental image*. But because his allusion to his girlfriend (and maybe also his underwear, really) had pulled her mind off car maintenance and Ava and reminded her how she was a total freak who had been considering throwing him into a lip-lock not fifteen minutes earlier.

"Listen, if I was being weird before"—she started before she'd even made the conscious decision to speak—"I don't know. I think I'm just weirded out by the whole stranded-in-a-snowstorm thing."

He sat up straighter. "Me too! Precisely. I apologize if I . . . I didn't mean to be too familiar or anything. I mean, we hardly know each other."

"Right, true! We hardly know each other!"

Well, if there had been any question, there was her answer. She'd been right, he had no interest in her beyond basic human decency. Of course he didn't. Her and her stupid brain.

It was getting cold already and would get colder as the remaining heat left the car and the overnight temperatures dropped even farther. In the romantic comedy version of these events, this would be where they'd huddle together for warmth.

But if Sabrina had learned one thing, it was that life was *not* a romantic comedy.

"We should try to stay as warm as possible," she said, retucking the pajama bottoms she wore into the slipper socks to try to keep her body heat in.

"Right, yes," he said, scooting just a little farther into his own corner, away from her.

## CHAPTER FIFTEEN

*N*oah pulled his jacket around him, doing up the buttons. He had thought Ava was warming up to him. In fact, he had thought—but obviously he was wrong.

Right, well, there you go. If he had needed any further proof this woman—who, it should be remembered, had begun their time together by glaring at him—did not have a romantic interest in him, there it was.

And he had none in her either. So. Good. That was that.

Although they did now have to spend the next however long until they were rescued together in this small space.

She offered him a tiny smile. "You said you like camping. Is this the kind of roughing it you like?"

"Generally, I would have avoided camping in these conditions."

She chuckled, her smile widening, lighting up her face.

If he was honest, it was hard not to notice how pretty she looked. Despite, or maybe because of, her current state of disarray. His extra clothes were layered on top of hers, way, way too big for her. She had taken off the chauffeur's hat, and her blonde curls, ruffled by the chaos of the day, now seemed to want to go every which way. Her cheeks, he could just see in the dim light, had flushed as the heat slowly dissipated from the car and the cold took over.

Maybe if he got lucky, she'd start laying into him again about something. He found it strangely enjoyable when she insulted him. It made him want to spar with her, get the better hand, or maybe sweep her into his arms and—

All right. Perhaps he was a little attracted to her. But it made no difference. It was all wrong.

She wasn't interested, for one thing. And he had a girlfriend—at least in theory—for another. *And* he had his very public personal life and the reputation of the company to think about.

The press loved him and Victoria together (hell, they had basically created a him and Victoria from thin air). And he and Ava barely knew each other. And he wasn't thinking straight because of all that was weighing on him. Not to mention, they *had* just been in a car accident.

No. He needed to be cool and calm. Responsible. Practical. For the company, his parents, all the employees. And most of all for Ava.

The only thing she needed less than a guy so full of himself he threw himself at her despite her obvious lack of interest was a guy *too messed up to know what he wanted* throwing himself at her despite her obvious lack of interest.

Although, looking at her now, he'd say what she needed most of all was a blanket.

See? This was exactly what daydreaming brought you.

He had been so caught up in his thoughts he hadn't even noticed she was freezing. Which was anything *but* responsible.

"Are you okay?" he asked her.

"Not really. You?"

He thought about it. Actually, his fingers had gone numb. "We could start the car again."

"I'm guessing that won't work for another half hour or so. And even then probably not for very long." She took a deep breath and let it out slowly.

What she was saying was the heat wouldn't be enough to keep them warm that night. There was one obvious choice. Really, it was their only choice.

He shrugged. "Well. Under the circumstances . . ."

"Yeah, okay."

She was relatively ensconced in her corner, injured leg stretched out across the floor, so he scooted over toward her. He took off his car coat and spread it over the both of them like a blanket. His arm fell naturally around her shoulders, and he drew her close. She stiffened for a second before resting against his chest, her head tucked under his chin.

Her breathing slowed as she relaxed into him.

They were just doing what was practical, given the situation.

And he would just have to ignore that he was enjoying it.

~

SABRINA KNEW NOAH WAS RIGHT. She might have preferred not to be snuggling with him under this makeshift blanket, but it was better than freezing to death.

So much better.

He wrapped his arms a little tighter around her. It would be easy to imagine that meant something—especially with her deeply troubled and overactive imagination —but it obviously didn't.

Just one human being doing the decent thing and trying to keep another human safe in dropping temperatures. Not even. He benefited just as much from their shared warmth as she did.

She cuddled closer against him. Which was a totally reasonable thing to do. Because warmth.

So. There they were. Sitting in the dark, cuddling. Mere minutes after she almost jumped him.

Okay, maybe she hadn't almost *jumped* him, but if she had to stay pressed up against him like this, smelling his woodsy, masculine smell, hearing his slow, steady breath, hell, feeling his heart beating for God's sake—she just might. She might have sworn off fairy-tale men, the universe might be testing her . . . but there was only so much a girl could take.

God, was she glad he couldn't see her face.

It was going to be a long, long night. Somehow this felt both too awkward and not awkward enough.

Finally, Noah broke the silence. "So, obviously, this is a little strange."

Sabrina couldn't help it, she burst out laughing.

Then *he* started laughing. Low, happy rumbles that came from deep in his chest, which she felt as much as she heard. And so help her, she wanted to kiss him all over again.

"Well," he said, "I have to tell you it's been one of my more interesting days. No matter what happens, I think it's safe to say I won't be forgetting you anytime soon, Ava."

The name hung in the air. There they were, all cozied up, sharing this experience, getting to know each other, at least in a way.

He had carried her back from the road, worried about her being concussed, shared his secret Cheese Doobers with her. Now he was spending the night cold and stranded, just trying to keep her warm.

And she was lying to him.

They had each already shared secrets. And yet. She was keeping this huge one. It didn't seem right.

And suddenly, she just couldn't anymore. She made a silent wish to the universe not to let this come down on Ava's head (it seemed pretty clear Noah Prince wasn't about complaining about the help and getting them fired).

She pulled back a few inches, turning her face to his.

"Actually, my name isn't really Ava."

## CHAPTER SIXTEEN

*F*or a split second, Noah had wondered if he should worry about her head again. She had seemed lucid since the accident, though, truth be known, he'd still been keeping an eye on her for symptoms.

But when she explained that she had just lied to take her roommate's place, all he could do was laugh.

"You're not mad?" She seemed genuinely worried.

Probably because he could turn them in to the car company. Although, if she'd been that worried about it, she could have just kept up the lie. Was it too much to hope that maybe she wanted to tell him the truth . . . for personal reasons?

"That you broke the rules to give your friend a little quality time with her boyfriend? No."

Maybe he should be mad at her, but he couldn't. He found it fairly endearing, actually.

"Well, it wasn't just because of that. Remember that ex-boyfriend I told you about?"

She explained that this horrible ex had actually taken

her proposal—the one she'd confided in him she dreamed of—and used it on his new girlfriend.

"On the plus side, it was really a pretty clichéd proposal. I could never, for instance, use it in a script. Way too hackneyed."

She was trying to make light of it, but he could hear the hurt in her voice.

He was furious anyone could do this to her. How could they? And not just the emotional pain, the cheap shot of stealing her dream proposal. He could see now—she'd gone from watching *Happily Ever Valentine*, writing romantic comedies, and wistful romantic fantasies to dismissing it all as nonsense. She'd lost her idealism. She didn't believe in fairy-tale endings. Just because some jackass was too thick to see what an amazing person she was.

"That guy's an idiot, you know that, right?"

He gave her a squeeze.

All right, he liked her. He really liked her. But what did that matter?

It couldn't go anywhere. He couldn't imagine how messy it would be to drag her into his circus (for which she had expressed disdain, after all). And being with someone so outspoken, so . . . well, not from the same circles he normally socialized in . . . That posed potential problems for him as well.

Pursuing any kind of relationship with Av—*Sabrina*—would be asking for trouble. Any reasonable person would steer clear, no matter what they felt for her.

For that matter, any reasonable person in his position would head right back into the city in the morning, tell

Victoria they were sorry, and immediately start planning their wedding with her.

There was only one problem. He didn't want to marry Victoria.

BRADY *WAS* AN IDIOT. It was part of why it bothered her so much that he got to her. So, yes, she did know that.

"I could beat him up for you, if you wanted," Noah teased gently. She couldn't suppress her smile.

She loved that he was defending her.

She couldn't afford to love it, though. Especially not pressed up against him for warmth in a dark car in the middle of nowhere. Not if she wanted to keep herself from thinking things she absolutely wanted to keep herself from thinking.

She changed the subject.

"So . . . how much not to tell anyone you don't know how to pop the hood on one of these babies?"

He feigned outrage. "You didn't know either!"

"Yeah, and now you know why. I've never driven one before. But I thought all you rich guys were all about the fancy cars."

"Well, first of all, I think that's more race cars and sexier things like that." She was just going to ignore how sexy it was to hear him say "sexy." "But also . . . okay, this one is a real secret." He whispered, "I don't actually drive."

"Right, because you have drivers."

"Well, yes. But I have drivers because I can't drive. I don't know how."

"What?!" She half screamed, half laughed.

"I grew up in the city. Traffic is insane. And . . . I was lucky enough not to need to, so . . ."

Okay, this was hilarious. And adorable. She liked these kinds of details so much better than any standard princely type stuff.

"I probably shouldn't tell a writer all my secrets," he said with a laugh.

"Don't worry, I wouldn't—"

"I know," he said softly, and they fell quiet again.

But the revelation made her think (sometimes she hated how she couldn't turn her mind off). If she wrote him as a character, she had to admit (begrudgingly), it would be as a romantic lead. *Not* because of his obvious and well-lauded attributes, but because of things like not knowing how to drive.

He was sweet. He was not perfect. He was *real*. At least, he was real to her now.

And if she was honest, that made him infinitely more appealing . . . both on and off the page.

But she was not going to go *there*.

Still, *on* the page was something she could contemplate. And the more time she spent with him, the more she had to admit he'd make for an intriguing character. Except, it occurred to her, if she were writing his character, there was one question she'd really want an answer to.

*Don't ask, don't ask, don't ask.*

"What's the deal with you and Victoria Ashby?" Great.

She felt him stiffen beside her and rushed to explain. "Sorry, I was just—it's a writer thing, I guess. Kind of a thought experiment."

And it was. She wasn't just being nosy. No. She was simply suddenly overcome with a need to understand what drove him, how his mind worked.

Why he would be with a woman if he didn't love her.

*If* he was actually with that woman.

That sort of thing.

As a *writer*.

"I guess that makes sense," said Noah with just slight hesitation. Thank God, because all the convincing herself was starting to be not so convincing. "Maybe it's a good way of looking at it. Clinical. More removed. Actually, maybe that's exactly what I need to do."

The feelings she was having were anything but clinical, but they weren't talking about her, and she had no intention of making that public anyway, so she just nodded.

Noah sighed. "I like Victoria."

Sabrina felt a pang in her chest. Right. Of course he did. He'd been seen all over the world with her for years now.

"But," he continued, "it's not the most passionate relationship."

And Sabrina's heart raced with hope, and she mentally told it to chill the hell out already. Should she say anything? Was it okay to ask more questions? She had questions.

Screw it. "What do you mean?"

He ran a hand through his hair.

"It's more of, I don't know, a business arrangement, maybe?" She must have looked shocked because he rushed to say, "In a good way. Or at least not a bad way."

Sabrina reminded herself that her new, non-romantic,

realist self should approve of looking at romance in practical terms.

But a business arrangement?

"Are you actually together?"

"We weren't. Then we were." He shrugged. "I don't know. It all happened without me really thinking about it. She's a good partner. Smart, pragmatic."

"And beautiful," she couldn't help but throw in.

He laughed. "Yes, that too. But—"

"But you don't love her."

Of course he didn't. He had already told her he had never been in love. But had she actually just said that out loud? Shoot her now.

Noah sighed and shook his head. "No."

Okay, then.

They were quiet for a minute. Just when she was starting to think of three-guys-walk-into-a-bar jokes to tell to get them away from this awkward silence, he began again.

"But her proposal still made sense. So far this arrangement has worked for us both. And it's easy."

"Easy?" Yeah, that sounded romantic.

Not that she cared about romance anymore, she reminded herself.

He tipped his head to the side, considering. "Not messy, like other relationships."

"Like me and Brady."

"Yes, I suppose. Although more like my brother and . . . everyone."

She laughed. "He does make the papers a lot."

He grinned, his perfect teeth still gleaming even in the low light. "So you can see why I'd want to avoid that."

"Well, sure. But all you really had to do was not get caught with the married daughter of East Asian royalty and you'd be fine. It's a pretty low bar, when you think about it."

He laughed hard at that, shaking his head. "A fair point. But I've always tried to do better than just clear the bar."

She could see that. It wasn't just that he gave the impression of a GQ model crossed with a Boy Scout. He had actual, genuine integrity. It was annoyingly charming.

"Okay, so she asked you to marry her."

He shifted in his seat. "She suggested we do, yes."

"So what are you going to do?"

She probably shouldn't ask, and she didn't really want to know, but she had to know, you know?

He sighed.

"I don't know. It's not that crazy, her suggestion. She made a compelling argument." He cracked a smile. "She had a checklist. Reasons we should get married."

And another thing she didn't really want to hear more about, but . . .

"Okay. So what was on the checklist?"

"We want the same things," he said, ticking it off on his fingers.

"Do you?"

"I don't know. Some of them, sure." He took a breath. "Then there was that we understand each other."

"And?"

He looked down. He looked *pained*. And all she could think to do was take away that pain as fast as she could.

"She doesn't know about your Cheese Doober obsession, does she?"

He shook his head and laughed. Better.

"Anything else?"

"We make sense." He said this with an air of finality and maybe a little resignation.

"Well, you kind of do."

"Sure we do. That's how we ended up together in the first place. We were friends from when we were young. When we grew up, we ran in the same circles. We started going to things because neither of us had someone to go with."

Realization slammed into her.

"And the media loved you."

~

NOAH SIGHED. "THEY DID. THEY DO."

Somewhere along the way, their arrangement had become a relationship (of sorts). Because it was easy. Because it was there.

They were both driven people who needed to maintain impeccable public profiles. They didn't have time for dating and drama and looking for "the one." They enjoyed each other's company. There hadn't been a clear reason *not to*.

And maybe they'd been a little lonely too.

Regardless of their reasons, it was fine. Their relationship was fine. Built, if nothing else, on mutual respect.

At least until he'd run out on her that morning.

He shook his head. He was a bastard, and a selfish one at that.

"There are quite a few reasons I ought to consider Victoria's proposition seriously."

It was true, even if it did make his stomach twist into a tight knot.

He was half waiting for her to make some sarcastic comment. He might have smiled if she had. He was getting used to them, finding them endearing even.

"Maybe you shouldn't have run away." There was a bit of bite to her statement, but it was less snark and more . . . hurt. Almost like she was jealous. But when she spoke again, it was gone, and he was sure he must have imagined it.

"I'm sure you'll figure it out," she said.

"Yes, I suppose I will."

Yes. He sighed.

In the silence that followed, his mind started putting *her* through Victoria's checklist. Did they want the same things? He suspected they both longed for love and acceptance in the same secret way, neither expecting it would happen. Did they understand each other? He felt, oddly, in the small (and frankly not entirely honest) time they'd spent together that maybe they did. Not in the big, generalized, I've-got-your-number kind of way people usually meant when they talked about that sort of thing. But in the tiny, seemingly insignificant details they had shown each other, maybe because they didn't know each other, didn't expect their paths to cross again.

Did they make sense? Not at all. And that, in its own

messy, illogical, mixed-up way, maybe made more sense than anything else.

She settled against him, and they were quiet for a long time. He could feel her relaxing. It was early, but it had been a long, exhausting day.

"So you really don't know what you're going to do?" she asked sleepily.

"I have no idea." And that was the truth.

She hadn't spoken in so long he thought she had drifted off to sleep, but then she said softly, "Noah?"

"Yes?"

"You deserve to be happy, you know that, right?"

Perhaps, but it was so much more complicated than that. He had so many responsibilities. A whole company counting on him, his parents, the foundation, and the charities it supported too. And, truly, the whole world was watching.

Even if he *had* some inkling of what would make him happy, he wasn't sure it was fair to go for it. To take a chance just to serve his own needs.

And chances sometimes didn't work out. There was that, too, if he was honest.

But he was touched beyond measure that she would say such a thing to him. When people held your life up as the example of perfect, well, they rarely thought to consider your happiness.

He still wasn't sure what he was going to do.

There was one thing he was quite sure of, however.

"You deserve to be happy, too, Sabrina."

CHAPTER SEVENTEEN

*M*aybe it had been a mistake to tell him her real name. Not because he could get her and Ava in a lot of trouble with Ava's employer (and, considering the accident, quite possibly their insurance company and maybe the law). No.

Because hearing him whisper her name in the darkness like that, the two of them pressed together, their body heat mingling (and, fine, keeping them alive) . . . well, it was almost more than she could bear.

Except he was seriously considering marrying an heiress/business icon/philanthropist/Miss Universe contender (okay, that last one was metaphorical). And Sabrina had sworn off dreaming of handsome princes.

Not that she would have dreamed one like Noah. She shifted against him, wishing she could get some space between them, but the whole avoiding hypothermia thing got in the way. That and the fact that she very much did not want to get space between them.

Ugh.

How was she supposed to swear off romantic fantasy men when she was clinging to one for dear life? Unfair, universe! Unfair.

She had given up hope that a plow would come by anytime soon. The road was so dark, with its few scattered streetlamps, she didn't know if anyone would even notice their "flags" if they did come by.

As if on cue, the little light they had, spilling in from those streetlamps, blinked off. The power must have gone out. Of course.

At this point, she might as well resign herself to this until morning. They could probably turn the car on again soon . . . and run it for about five minutes before the safety shut it off again. Hardly even worth it.

Yup. She was stuck here snuggling Prince Charming for the night, whether she liked it or not.

She refused to think about how much she liked it.

And she was tired. Tired of fighting her stupid brain, tired of fighting the universe, tired of this whole day that had gone so wrong. Tired of working so hard to dislike this guy she actually kind of liked.

And more than a little afraid that if she opened her mouth again, she was going to clue him into that.

But this even darker darkness only served to make the silence feel even *more* intimate. Which was no good.

"So." She offered feebly.

She felt rather than heard him laugh. Along her side. Against her ear.

He cleared his throat, sounding almost as uncomfortable as she felt. "We could, um . . ."

"Sit here in awkward silence?"

This time she heard the laugh. A great, low, rumbling laugh that made her stomach flip. Bad stomach. Bad, bad stomach.

"Oh!" said Noah, sitting up slightly so that cold air rushed to fill the new space between them. He pulled his phone from his suit pocket. "How about a podcast?"

"Yes! Yes! Excellent idea!" she said. And thank God, because the next second he settled back next to her, closing that gap between them and even wrapping his arm more tightly around her (because he was trying to keep them from freezing to death), and she needed all the help she could get.

SABRINA'S BREATHING became deep and even, and he felt her relax against his chest. It was probably the longest she'd gone without insulting him since he'd met her.

Noah smiled to himself in the dark. With no signal, they could only listen to the podcasts he already had downloaded on his phone. Financial reports and Wall Street analysis had put her right to sleep.

He had turned down the volume so as not to disturb her, and aside from the continued droning voices in the background, all was still. He was struck by the isolation. He traveled to the house to get away. From work, from the chaos of the city, from social obligations, from all his responsibilities.

But he never really felt free of them. Not like this.

Maybe it was the surrounding forest or the dark or the storm. Maybe the sheer strangeness of the situation. But what had started as one of the most overwhelming days he'd ever had, had ended in such comfortable quiet, he just wanted to sink into it and stay there.

Sabrina shifted, threatening to tumble onto the car floor, and he wrapped his arms around her tighter, pulling her to him. She mumbled something incoherent that sounded a little like "mayonnaise," and he had to stifle a laugh.

And then suddenly he was caught with such affection for her that he almost couldn't breathe. She was so . . . smart-mouthed, argumentative, sweet, generous, stubborn, confusing. There had been no dull moments with Sabrina today, and he had a feeling that might be the case most days, in fact.

That should have been a scary thought, but instead, it only made him like her more.

Could he be with someone like this? Just hypothetically, if he allowed himself to imagine it, could he?

The tabloids would have a field day. The photos of her hair alone, untamed and haphazard as she strode on his arm through some charity event or other. Never mind if she actually spoke to the press. He imagined her on magazine covers, "Prince Charming's Opinionated Cinderella" or something like that.

He smiled at the thought. The media would probably love her, actually. She'd certainly liven things up. Which might be bad for the company. As long as he was fantasizing, though, he could also allow for the possibility it wouldn't be so bad.

But what about her? Would she want that kind of attention? He doubted it, though he also couldn't imagine her letting it get to her. She certainly seemed to be a woman of conviction. If she didn't like something, she would probably just leave.

What if she left?

What if he poured his heart and soul into pursuing something with this woman he had only just met—a real relationship, with passions and feelings and not just practical choices? What if he went out on a limb like that, put it all on the line—the company reputation, his future, his *heart*—and it blew up?

What if the whole messy, uncontrollable thing just blew up in his face?

"Marshmallow," Sabrina murmured against his neck.

Noah's heart squeezed, and all the thoughts swirling through his head gave way to just one: Maybe it would still be worth it. Hypothetically, of course.

CHAPTER EIGHTEEN

*S*abrina blinked as she woke to the glare of sunlight reflected off the snow. Her breath clouded in the air in front of her, disappearing as it floated off through the inside of the car. Yup, it was still freaking cold.

Neither the light nor the freezing temperature seemed to be bothering Noah, though, whose chest rose and fell with deep, steady breaths as she leaned against it. His arms were wrapped tightly around her.

Which felt a little too good, but fortunately she didn't have time to contemplate it because, oh God, did she need to pee.

Noah must have snuck off one of those times he had ventured outside the car without her. Or maybe billionaires didn't have to pee like mere mortals. But for her . . . yeah, this was an emergency.

She eased her way out slowly. She could have just woken him, but she didn't really feel like discussing this particular issue with him.

Finally, she managed to free herself. She wished she had actual shoes she could wear—well, ski boots, as long as she was wishing—but Noah's slipper socks would have to do. At least they had rubberized soles.

Once outside, she limped off, carefully picking her way through the twelve-plus inches of new snow. Fortunately, her ankle seemed to have improved overnight, so walking, while not easy, was bearable. And she was pleasantly surprised to find that, with the sun shining down and no breeze in the air, it wasn't any colder outside than it had been in the car.

She went a decent distance and then behind a huge evergreen tree, careful to make sure she could see neither the car nor the road from her spot. There was *no* way she was risking a handsome billionaire witnessing her squatting in the woods. The road was still covered in thick snow, so there probably wasn't anyone coming along that way anytime soon either, but just in case. She wondered how long it would be until the plows made it through. Ava must be worried sick.

These were still not exactly ideal circumstances in which to drop trou, but beggars couldn't be choosers. Just as she was finishing up her business, something caught her eye in the distance, through the trees.

Her eyes went wide, and she struggled to pull up her pants as fast as she could.

As she fumbled with the fabric, she screamed, "Noah!"

~

NOAH WOKE WITH A START.

It was cold. It was bright. Where was he? Oh, yes.

And where was Sabrina?

"Noaaaah!"

He looked around frantically through the windows but couldn't find her anywhere.

"Nooooaaaaah!"

She sounded far off. And almost frenzied, like something was going on. Like—

What if she was hurt?

"Noah!!!"

He leapt out of the car so fast he stumbled to the ground. Random items spilled out from inside—his phone, the empty Cheese Doobers bag, her broken shoe. He stuffed them into his pockets and ran toward the sound of her voice, struggling to keep his balance in the snow.

"Sabrina! Sabrina, where are you?"

He didn't see her anywhere. Maybe he had gone the wrong way. Fear flooded his brain. What had she done? She'd already been injured and now—his stomach twisted. He had to find her. He *had* to.

If she was hurt, if—

He froze for a second as realization hit. How he was feeling was not hypothetical at all.

He cared about this woman, this crazy woman who glared at him and climbed mountains in heels against his advice and whose real name he hadn't known until late last night. Cared about her in a way he wasn't sure he'd ever cared about anyone before. In that ill-advised, messy, weak-in-the-knees sort of way he'd made himself think he'd be fine without.

"Noah! Over here!"

He turned his head to see her limping toward him faster than he thought she should, given her ankle. But she seemed otherwise fine. Thank God.

In fact, she was grinning from ear to ear.

He hurried toward her, and when they met, she grabbed onto both his hands, steadying herself. She was laughing.

"What are you doing?" He was still breathing heavily from the run, and it came out sounding almost panicked.

She knit her brows. "You okay there, champ?"

Was he? He wasn't sure. He nodded anyway.

She cocked her head to the side, reached up, and touched his hair, which he could feel was sticking up in several directions. She cracked a smile. "So, this is what Prince Charming looks like in the morning, eh?"

He wanted to be mad at her. For disappearing without telling him. For looking so adorable in his huge sweater, cheeks flushed and eyes sparkling.

There was no way he could be mad at her. "Why were you calling me?"

She grinned wider, grabbed onto his shoulders, and spun him around. There, through the trees, maybe a quarter-mile away, was a cozy little house, complete with smoke coming out of the chimney.

Which meant someone was home.

Which meant . . .

"They'll let us use their phone, right?" Sabrina asked. "I mean, we do look a little scraggly, but come on, wayward travelers in need?"

Of course they needed to use the phone. Call a tow truck, call her friend, and sort out the business with the car company. Get on with their days. With their lives.

But he couldn't help it. He didn't really want this adventure to end.

"Yeah, yeah, I'm sure they will."

He had tried to sound enthusiastic, but Sabrina's expression faded, and he knew he hadn't. Maybe she wasn't looking forward to their "rescue" either?

He bumped his arm into hers. "This is good, right? Back to civilization? We'll be able to change into regular clothes and eat something other than Cheese Doobers."

She gave him a little smile, and his heart swelled.

They stared at each other a moment longer, the clouds of their breath mingling in the air in front of them. But what else was there to say?

"Okay, then! Let's go!" And with that, she turned and began limping over the uneven terrain in his slipper socks toward the house.

He called after her. "You shouldn't be walking on that ankle!"

"I'm fine," she shouted, not turning around or slowing down.

Noah shook his head and smiled. There was no way he was letting her do that.

SABRINA SQUEALED as Noah scooped her off her feet.

"What are you doing?"

"I can't have you reinjuring that ankle, no matter how certain you are of your own medical opinion."

He didn't carry her delicately like yesterday, but instead flung her over his shoulder fireman-style.

"Are you sure this isn't just your way of reasserting your manliness after you failed so spectacularly at automotive troubleshooting?"

"Quite possibly." He swung her around for good measure.

Sabrina laughed. Secretly she relished the closeness. But this was necessary anyway since he was probably right about her ankle. Nothing wrong with taking necessary help. And if she squirmed and whacked at him playfully for his brutish treatment of her? That could be reasonable too, right?

As he tromped between the trees, she reached out and grabbed at a low-hanging branch, sending a giant blob of snow down on his head.

He threw a look at her over his shoulder and deadpanned. "Thank you."

Sabrina felt a pang all through her body.

She was going to miss this. She was going to miss *him*.

When they arrived at the front door of the lovely little cottage—connected, as they could now see, to the road by a winding driveway—he set her down gently on the stoop.

"Milady." He tipped an imaginary cap to her, then turned and knocked on the door.

There were lights in the windows, peeking out from behind the curtains. From inside, they heard an elderly woman's voice. "Coming!" She sounded far off, like it may take her a while.

Noah reached a hand up to smooth back his hair, discovered the random flakes of snow still clinging up there, and gave his head a shake, sort of like a big dog. It was a candid moment, real and unpolished, and it was almost impossible not to get sucked in. Would it be so wrong to give in to the fantasy just for another hour or two?

He glanced up from under his swoon-worthy lashes and gave her a look that cut to her soul.

Yes, wrong. So wrong.

The door swung open, and a lovely white-haired woman about four and a half feet tall and 90 if she was a day smiled at them. "Yes?"

"So sorry to bother you, ma'am," said Sabrina, "but could we possibly use your phone?"

$\mathcal{T}$he woman, Gladys as she had introduced herself, threw another log on the fire while Sabrina used the phone in the den down the hall. Gladys was incredibly spry for her age and size.

"I'm just so happy I could help. To think of the two of you stranded out there in the storm!" She shook her head and *tsked*. She had, however, been kind enough not to comment on their state of dishevelment, for which Noah was grateful.

Sabrina's voice drifted through the small house, and he caught snippets of her conversation with Ava. Sabrina was apologizing profusely, but from the sound of it, Ava was far more concerned with her friend's safety than the situation with the car. He made a mental note to call the car company himself, to commend Sabrina's—Ava's—performance under difficult conditions. He knew his family had enough clout with the company that pleasing him ought to be sufficient motivation for them to let the accident go without any negative repercussions for Ava. As for her switching with Sabrina, he knew Sabrina didn't feel great about it either, but it was clear it was best if they just never found out. It would just be their little secret.

This whole experience, he realized, would be their little secret.

"It's been interesting," he heard Sabrina say. When he looked up, he caught her eyeing him from inside the open doorway, smiling. She quickly turned away. "About four hours? Sure, I could do that."

She stepped deeper into the room as they continued to work things out.

He was relieved it sounded like there was a plan to deal with the whole car situation. He needed to start thinking about his *own* plan. He'd need to get in touch with Victoria, of course. She was probably worried sick or furious or both, considering any attempts to contact him for the last day would have gone unanswered. As well as other questions that had gone unanswered . . .

He did not relish the idea of dealing with any of it. In truth, he'd prefer not to think about it at all. At least not now. Not while he had this tiny bit of time left in this sort of alternate world he'd fallen into.

"How about some tea, dear?"

Gladys smiled up at him, bringing him back to the present.

"Oh, no, thank you. I don't want to put you to any trouble."

She waved a dismissive hand. "It's no bother. Come, help me."

She led the way into her tiny kitchen. Sunshine

streamed through floral curtains, making the room bright and warm.

She put a kettle on the stove, and he helped her get down tea bags and china cups from the cabinets. He could still hear Sabrina on the phone off in the den, though from in here he couldn't make out the words.

"I like your girlfriend, there," said Gladys. "She's a fire-cracker."

He wondered how Gladys had picked up on that so quickly, but she wasn't wrong. Sabrina certainly was a "firecracker."

His girlfriend.

He smiled at the thought. Just a guy having car trouble, out with his girlfriend. Could that be him? Could life be that simple?

There didn't seem to be much point in correcting her. He was kind of enjoying not being recognized, actually. That didn't happen too often these days.

"I like this one way more than the last one," she added. The last one? "Don't get me wrong, that Victoria seems very smart and elegant, but I just didn't see any passion between you two."

So much for not being recognized. And yet she still thought he and Sabrina were together, even with his very well-publicized relationship still going strong (at least as far as anyone other than he and Victoria—and Sabrina—knew). What had made her think that? He'd missed the Pink Heart Ball, but he doubted this woman followed New York society so closely as to have heard that already. And even if she had, it hardly meant . . .

"Why do you—" He cleared his throat and began again. "How did you know Sabrina and I were . . ."

She patted his hand. "You two are such a sweet pair. I can see it in your eyes—you really like each other."

He'd be lying if he said that wasn't true, at least on his part. Or if he said he didn't hope it was true on hers as well. Gladys poured hot water over tea bags, and he leaned out into the hall to catch a glimpse of Sabrina. She was still on the phone, turned away from him, fingers absently combing through her hair, futilely trying to tame it.

"If I were you, I wouldn't let this one go." Somehow Gladys had snuck up on him. She was right behind him, peering around to watch Sabrina. He turned back to her.

"I will keep that in mind."

"Good." She patted his arm. "Now help me get the good cookies down from the shelf."

He did as she asked. Both the cookies and the keeping Sabrina in mind. He had a feeling he couldn't *not* do that if he tried.

~

WHEN SABRINA STEPPED into the kitchen, Noah looked up and smiled at her. Like *really* smiled at her. She had no idea why. But it made her stomach do a little flip.

She filled him in on her conversation with Ava. How Ava had already covered with the car company by calling last night (after she couldn't reach Sabrina on her phone) and telling them she couldn't make it back till today because of the storm. Plus, their plan for Ava to come up on the train so she could deal with the repairs (as an official company representative). They'd have to fudge the part about when/how the accident had occurred since Ava hadn't mentioned it when she'd called in, but they thought it would work.

Sabrina was a little uncomfortable talking about all this in front of the old woman, but Gladys just puttered around putting cookies on a plate and humming to herself. It sounded like "Love Is a Many-Splendored Thing."

"Anyway, I called for a tow truck. They said it would be here in an hour. Although it will be longer if the roads aren't cleared by then."

As if on cue, there was a rumbling outside. They all three looked out the window to see a big orange plow go past. Was it wrong Sabrina had secretly wished it might take them a little longer?

"Or maybe not." Time to get back to reality. Nothing about that seemed appealing.

Gladys gasped. "Isn't that wonderful! Now you two can get back to your romantic getaway!"

Sabrina gave Noah a look, but he shook his head. Apparently, he had already decided not to disabuse their hostess of this misconception.

"But first, sit down, have a cookie. Indulge a little old lady. You two are just the cutest couple."

Sabrina hesitated, but only for an instant. She smiled, taking a seat at the little table Gladys had put the food on. "Thank you."

If she was going to indulge in a fantasy, she might as well enjoy it a little while longer. She'll have to go back to her real life soon enough.

As they ate, she looked over at Noah. Gladys must not

have recognized him, or he wouldn't be at ease like this, letting her think they were a couple. He caught her watching and grinned before taking his cookie, dunking it messily into his tea, then shoving it into his mouth. He waggled his brows at her. She had to suppress a laugh so as not to spray cookie crumbs everywhere.

He seemed so relaxed, comfortable, like there was nowhere else in the world he'd rather be.

The thought sent a thrill through her. Was that possible? Sure, compared to her regular life, being stranded with a billionaire made for a pretty extraordinary experience no matter how you sliced it. But was there a chance spending the last day with her had been remarkable to him too?

Their eyes met across the table; he smiled at her. Maybe it *was* possible.

She knew one thing: no matter how she had tried to resist, with that kind of look? There was no point in denying it anymore. She was a goner.

God help her. What was she supposed to do with that?

## CHAPTER TWENTY

"Yep, you're gonna need a new radiator," the mechanic said, having required all of three minutes and one quick look at the undercarriage to make the diagnosis. "I'll hitch her up to the truck and tow you in. I'm just going to need a credit card."

Sabrina looked nervous. "It's for, um, my employer. Could they pay you after the fact?"

The guy sighed. "Lady—"

Noah pulled out his wallet and handed him his Visa. "Here you go." The guy nodded, then headed back to the truck to run the card.

"You didn't have to do that," she said, but she sounded relieved.

"I'll talk to the company too. Make sure they know the accident wasn't your—wasn't *Ava's* fault."

"I don't want to involve you. I'd feel terrible making you lie."

"I'm happy to keep your secret. I do have one condition." He leaned over and whispered, "You must never—

never ever—tell another living soul about my obsession with Cheese Doobers."

She laughed, and he realized how much he liked her laugh. How much he was going to miss it.

Even if it was scary or not the appropriate time or a thousand other excuses, if he didn't do or say something now, that would be it. She'd go back to her writing and her roommate and her idiot ex-boyfriend who still lived in the building, and he'd never see her again.

"Okay," said the tow truck driver, handing back his card, "I'll just hook you up to the rig, and we'll be good to go."

Was this really going to be it?

With sudden certainty, Noah knew. He didn't want it to be.

But if that was the case, he was going to need to do something about it.

SITTING between Noah and the driver in the cab of the tow truck, Sabrina watched the scenery roll by from under the brim of her chauffeur's cap. Everything looked cozy and quaint, covered in a thick layer of new snow. They'd passed a few small shops a few miles back, dug out and open for business. The storm had come and gone, and people were getting back to their lives.

She sighed, playing absently with her red blouse, now sitting in her lap. Noah had retrieved their things from the tree by the side of the road where he had tied them. His silk tie had snagged, leaving loose threads dangling from the branch, but he'd been much more careful with her shirt, and it had come out undamaged. Almost as if none of this had ever happened.

It had happened, though. As much as she'd sworn she wouldn't let herself get swept up, she had done just that, in the worst possible way.

She stole a glance at Noah.

In the best possible way.

Now what? She'd told herself she wouldn't indulge in any more fantasies. But what if it wasn't a fantasy?

That was crazy.

Wasn't it?

Then again, the way he had spoken to her last night, joked around with her this morning . . . had looked at her in the woman's house and . . . She glanced back at him again. The way he was looking at her now, actually.

They both looked away quickly.

"It's just down here about a mile," Noah told the driver, pointing to a side street.

The truck turned and started down the narrow road. They passed houses set back on wooded lots. Soon they would be at *his* house. Was this going to be it?

She looked over at his profile, a day's worth of scruff roughing up the lines of his otherwise perfect jawline, and suddenly she could push the thought away no longer. She knew, beyond a shadow of a doubt.

She didn't want this to be it.

But that was her. What did he want? Was it even possible he felt what she did? Should she try to find out? Was she *insane* for even considering it? Would she regret it if she didn't? What if she really was just getting duped by the fantasy yet again? Or . . .

What if this was as real as it felt and she was just too scared to take the chance?

"Up here, on the right." Noah nodded toward a dirt drive marked by a mailbox. His house must be down behind the thick growth of trees. Whoever he'd hired to maintain the place had already cleared the snow, so the truck turned down the path with relative ease. They'd be there in a second.

It was now or never.

"Noah . . ." He looked up, meeting her eyes. Searching them. She took a deep breath, and—

Something seemed to catch his eye outside. He froze.

"Mom?"

She turned to see a lovely middle-aged woman standing just outside the front door of a modest wood cabin dressed in a robe, her arms wrapped around herself for warmth. She wore a look of concern as she watched the truck pull to a stop in the circular drive in front of the house. Sabrina recognized her immediately as Cheryl Prince. A second later the equally recognizable figure of Noah's father, Warren Prince, joined her, also still in his nightclothes.

Noah turned to Sabrina. "I'll be right back."

Then he swung the door wide and rushed out to join his parents.

"Noah, sweetheart, what are you doing here? What happened? Oh, look at you!" His mother gestured to his haphazard appearance before wrapping him in a hug. "Oh, we were so worried! Victoria called and said she couldn't reach you on the phone all night. And we couldn't believe you'd miss the Pink Heart Ball!"

She craned around behind him to look at Sabrina. "Is someone with you?"

"Yes, I—"

"She's just the driver, Cheryl," his dad cut him off, "see the hat?"

Sabrina reached up and touched Ava's hat absently. Right.

She leaned out and pulled the truck door shut. Because they needed their privacy. Because she was intruding.

She felt a vibration and glanced down at the seat beside her, where Noah had left his phone. It must have finally connected to the cell network. It was blowing up with text notifications from Victoria Ashby.

*Noah, honey, where are you?*

*I feel awful about how we left things at breakfast, please let's talk.*

*Please let me know you're all right. I'm worried about you.*

The tow truck driver glanced down at the screen. He chuckled, looking at Sabrina. "Ooh, looks like Prince Charming's in trouble with the Little Princess."

She looked back at Noah, standing with his parents, people whose money and status radiated off of them, even in their pajamas. He looked like he belonged with them. He *did* belong with them. And his father was right. She was just the driver.

This was Noah's world, not hers. She, in fact, wasn't even his driver. She was his nothing. And she had not only let herself fall for him, she'd half convinced herself he might be falling for her. Because he'd chatted with her while they were stranded together. Because he'd been nice enough not to let her freeze to death.

But.

There would never be anything between them. There *could* never be anything between them. Of course there couldn't. He was Prince Charming. And she was an idiot.

IT WAS LOVELY that his parents had decided on a spontaneous Valentine's getaway, but it was rather inconvenient, considering he really needed some time with Sabrina. He'd better go talk to her.

"Mom, Dad, would you excuse me for a second?"

"Of course, dear, I'll go make you some breakfast," said his mom.

Behind him he could hear them talking.

"A tow truck. The boy arrives in a tow truck," said his dad. "This is why I only trust our personal drivers."

"Warren," scolded his mom.

He'd have to speak to them. Make sure his dad didn't call the car company and complain. Let them know what was going on with him. But first, he needed to see if what he hoped was going on was, in fact, going on. He knocked on Sabrina's window.

She rolled it down. He offered a self-conscious smile.

"Sorry about that. So, surprise! My parents are here."

"Of course. I'll just get out of your way." She handed him his phone. "Here. I think you have some new texts."

He shoved the phone into his pocket without looking at it.

"What? No! I—I had hoped . . . What I mean is, I was going to ask you if you wanted to come in. I mean, I'd been planning—but now I guess things have changed a bit . . ." He rubbed the back of his neck and tried again. "Look, my mother is making some food. Which I should warn you probably won't be very good, but we can always sneak out for Cheese Doobers later. I would love it if you would join us."

He offered her a hopeful smile.

She wouldn't quite meet his eye. "I should go."

"Sabrina, I—"

"It was very nice to meet you. I'm sorry about . . . well, everything." She pulled his bags from the floor of the cab, where they had stashed them, and handed them over. Then she looked down at her hands.

Nice to meet him?

He didn't understand. He wanted to talk to her. He had so much to say. He'd thought—

But . . . it didn't matter. She clearly didn't want what he wanted.

She didn't want him.

Maybe it had been a crazy thought anyway. Maybe he'd imagined the whole thing.

The driver leaned past Sabrina to look at him.

"Look, I don't want to intrude here, but I got a guy back at the garage trying to track down a radiator for this thing and two more calls in for tows."

"Of course, sorry. Well." He didn't want to say goodbye. He didn't want this to be it. But, if that's what she wanted, then that was that. He looked at Sabrina. "I . . . will give the car company a call and let them know their driver did an excellent job in a difficult situation."

She glanced up into his eyes. For just a second he could swear he saw something there, but then it was gone. She tucked a loose strand of hair behind her ear. "Thanks, I appreciate that. And your clothes . . . okay if I get them cleaned and send them back to you later in the week?"

"Sure," he managed. "Thank you."

"Okay."

"Okay. Um . . ." He leaned in awkwardly to hug her at the same time she offered her hand to shake. She let out a little self-conscious laugh before hugging him.

His face pressed into her hair, and he breathed in the smell. Lilacs, maybe. He tried to memorize it, then forced himself to pull away. She wasn't interested. Enough.

"Promise me you'll have that ankle looked at by an actual doctor, will you?"

"I'll consider it."

She said it flatly. He couldn't tell if she was serious or if that was an attempt at humor. The situation felt humorless.

"Noah?" his mother called from behind him. "Come eat, sweetheart, you must be starved."

There were so many things he hadn't said.

"Goodbye, Noah Prince." Sabrina rolled up the window and nodded to the driver, who began easing the truck slowly through the turnaround.

Noah held up a hand and waved as they continued out onto the road.

Then he turned and followed his mother into the house, because what else could he do?

$\mathcal{S}$abrina hobbled out of the apartment, locking the door behind her. The air cast the clinic doctor had told her to wear was awkward and not exactly the height of fashion, but mostly she disliked it because it was a constant reminder of that night in the woods. Good thing she only needed to wear it a couple of days.

She pushed the button for the elevator and checked her watch. Plenty of time to get to her temp job for the day. She was glad she'd gotten called in. She could use the distraction as much as the money (and she could definitely use the money).

The elevator arrived, and she eased on next to a woman with her nose in a magazine.

There was a certain billionaire on the cover, glossy and coiffed, staring back at her with gorgeous brown eyes. Of course. Because the universe wasn't just going to let her forget her mistake.

Fine. Actually, it was just a helpful reminder she lived in a very different world than Noah Prince. She wasn't going to let it faze her. She was determined to go about her day. If only she could get her mind out of that car.

The elevator stopped on the fourth floor, and Brady stepped on. Just what she needed.

He stood next to her, noting the air cast. "Whoa. What happened?"

"Nothing."

She stared hard at the numbers, willing them to go down faster. He reached out and touched her arm.

"Hey," he said softly, "I still worry about you, you know?"

She expected to feel anger or, worse, warm squishy feelings she absolutely didn't want, but instead, she felt . . . nothing. Huh.

"Thank you. I'm really okay."

"Good."

Yup, nothing. Well, what do you know? Maybe she was actually over him. That was real progress.

She felt almost giddy. If she was over Brady, she'd better tell Noah so he knew he didn't need to beat him up anymore!

Noah.

She couldn't tell Noah anything. Why was he the first thing she thought of?

Ugh. She was over Brady because she had transferred all her unhealthy fixation to Noah. Of course.

This wasn't progress at all.

～

"Morning, Sally." The neatly dressed older woman looked up from her desk.

"Good morning, Mr. Prince. I wasn't sure you'd be coming in today. I heard you had quite an ordeal while you were out of town." Confusion must have shown on his face because she added, "With the car accident. Don't worry, nothing made it into the press."

He nodded. "Ah, yes. Good. Thank you, Sally."

He headed on into his office.

The truth was he wanted to work. He'd had a grueling couple of days. First there'd been the difficult talk with Victoria, then one with his parents about his public role going forward. He'd thought that would be difficult too, but it had actually ended pretty well. Of course they appreciated him not gallivanting across the gossip columns like his brother, but they had had no idea he felt so much personal responsibility. He guessed he'd put that pressure on himself. At any rate, they'd told him in no uncertain terms to live a little and not worry so much. He was going to try.

His mind flashed to Sabrina.

But for now, the best he could do was just work.

There was a knock on his doorframe. Sally entered with a stack of folders.

"Here are the files on the Milan property, Mr. Prince. I thought you'd want to see them."

"Thanks, Sally."

"Can I get you anything else, sir? Sparkling water? Something from *La Crêperie*?"

He considered for a moment. If he was living on his

own terms, he might as well start now. "How about the sparkling water and a bag of Cheese Doobers?"

"Cheese Doobers?" Sally blinked, looked as if she might say something more, then simply nodded. "Right away."

She stepped away, then leaned back in a moment later. "I like them too, sir," she whispered. She winked conspiratorially, then she was gone.

He smiled to himself. It was one tiny change, but it was a start.

He shrugged his car coat off, hanging it on the rack in the corner. His hand brushed something hard.

He reached into the pocket and pulled out Sabrina's shoe. He shook his head. It was almost as if the universe were conspiring to keep him from forgetting her.

As if that would ever happen.

## CHAPTER TWENTY-TWO

The week after Valentine's, Sabrina sat on the couch with a notepad trying desperately to come up with a workable idea for her showcase script. She was required to use two characters, one male and one female. Other than that, it was wide open, but she was struggling. All her brain wanted to do was write stupid romances starring Noah Prince. *Thanks a lot, brain.*

She groaned in frustration. Ava looked up from her phone (she'd been texting Ben all night—Sabrina was starting to wonder if she was going to need to look for a wedding gift and a new roommate soon).

"Maybe you should give him a chance."

"What?"

"Noah Prince, you should give him a chance."

She should never have told Ava anything about that night. Not that she had told her how she'd been feeling. No need to go out of her way to talk about how stupid she'd been. But Ava had grilled her enough that the basic bullet points (carrying her back to the car, sharing his sweater . . . huddling for warmth) of their time together had come out.

From there she had simply assumed that Sabrina must now be crushing on him majorly. Sabrina had taken the basic strategy of denying the idea, but Ava remained unconvinced. Worse. Ava had decided, based on Sabrina's account, that *he* might actually be interested in *her*. She supposed she couldn't blame her, since she herself had fallen into that trap. But just *no*. She needed her to drop it.

"Ava, we've been through this."

"But that was before." She grinned mischievously.

"Before what?"

Ava popped onto the couch beside her and held up her phone. "Before *NY Society* announced he'd broken up with Victoria Ashby!"

Sabrina blinked at the screen.

Ava leaned in. "They put out a press release. It's true."

So. He had actually done it.

"That's nice."

"That's *nice*?"

It was not nice. It was confusing. It was upsetting. It twisted her heart in a thousand different directions.

Random thoughts flashed through her head: *Poor Noah, that had to be hard! He's available! So what, it's got nothing to do with* you. *And you don't care anyway, remember?*

Maybe she would care if it weren't all too good to be true. If the thought of Noah Prince suddenly giving it all up to choose a wannabe playwright from Brooklyn one paycheck away from missing rent wasn't a total, ludicrous fairy tale.

He had figured out what he wanted, and he had made it

happen (which was great). He hadn't, however, she couldn't help noting, tracked her down to get in touch. Maybe he didn't want Victoria Ashby, but that sure as hell didn't mean he wanted her.

"Yeah, nice. I'm sure the single women of the world are rejoicing as we speak. Listen, Ava, I really need to work on this script. The showcase is coming up, and I've got nothing. Would you excuse me?"

Her friend studied her for a minute. She sighed. "Sure. Yeah, of course."

Ava retreated to the kitchen, and Sabrina turned back to her notepad. She tried to think of interesting characters and dramatic situations, but all she could think about was Noah Prince.

LATER THAT NIGHT, after Sabrina had given up any pretense of writing for the day, she sat in the living room, mentally exhausted but unable to sleep. Ava had gone to bed already, which was just as well, since Sabrina couldn't talk to her about anything that was on her mind. Not unless she wanted a barrage of gloating/impromptu matchmaking advice.

Hell, Ava would probably throw her in a cab and send her over to his building on the spot if she knew how she was really feeling.

This was doing her no good. She had to get out of her head.

She grabbed the remote and turned on the TV. It was

166 | LAURIE BAXTER

on ChikFlix. *Happily Ever Valentine* was playing. The proposal scene with all the stars.

Of course it was.

Sabrina groaned, burying her face in a throw pillow to muffle the sound so she wouldn't wake Ava.

~

"It's like they're shining just for us."

"Maybe they are."

Evelyn and John met in a passionate kiss, the music swelled, the credits rolled.

Noah flicked off the TV.

He really shouldn't have watched that. If he hadn't been thinking about Sabrina already . . . oh, who was he kidding? He hadn't been thinking about anything *but* Sabrina since she'd gone away that morning.

He paused, eyeing his laptop on the bedside table. He shouldn't. He'd resisted so far . . .

But apparently *Happily Ever Valentine* was enough to put him over the edge.

He grabbed the computer, opened a browser, and started searching.

He looked her up on Facebook, Instagram, and LinkedIn (private profile, no profile, and three Sabrina Hopewells, none within a 200-mile radius of New York and none under the age of 50 as far as he could tell).

He hunted around the theater sites and found a couple write-ups of shows she'd done and a writing contest she'd placed in.

He stared at the one visible photo on her Facebook

account far longer than he would have liked to admit. He considered actually getting a Facebook account just so he could send her a friend request (sought-after bachelor billionaires generally avoided being personally accessible on social media). But he didn't want to do that anyway. He *couldn't* do it.

If she'd wanted to get in touch, she would have. She knew where he lived, where he worked. He had even alerted Sally in case she called or even stopped by. She hadn't made contact because she didn't want contact, and he needed to respect that.

Still, he longed to do something. To at least let her know how much meeting her had meant to him.

He still had her shoe. He supposed he could track down her address and send that back with maybe some flowers? Would that be weird? Would it be *creepy*?

He chuckled when he thought how she would react to that. The writer in her would object vehemently. What kind of gesture is sending back a broken shoe?

But that got him thinking.

There was one thing he could do for her. He grabbed the phone and dialed.

EARLY THE NEXT MORNING, Sabrina was back at her station on the couch, forcing herself through scene-writing exercises, trying to get something workable for the showcase, which was fast approaching. Thank God it was only ten-minute plays, and they weren't expected to be polished. Still, she had just days to get her pages to the actors, and they couldn't be blank. If she didn't settle on an idea and get a draft roughed in today, she wasn't going to make it.

She had tried everything. Battle of wits. Criminal on the lam. Bear on the loose. But everything she tried ended up the same. She crumpled her latest attempt. A setup that was supposed to be a psychological thriller in the vein of *Rear Window*. Like all the others, the male lead had somehow morphed into a version of Noah and the characters had declared their undying passion and started making out.

Some writers loved it when their characters took on a life of their own. Right now, she wished hers would drop dead. Or at least shut up and do what they were told.

Ava emerged from her bedroom in full chauffeur uniform, ready to head off to work. Thank God everything had gone smoothly with the car company. Apparently, Noah had insisted on covering the cost of the repair, telling the company he felt responsible for requesting their service while forecasters were predicting the heavy storm. The company had been happy to agree, since it meant they didn't have to file an insurance claim and risk their rates going up. She and Ava had been happy, since it meant they weren't implicated in insurance fraud (a detail neither had thought of in their initial, somewhat panicked, plan for disaster control).

So rescued by the handsome prince, she supposed, yet again. She hated the idea, but for Ava's sake, she'd decided to just be grateful.

Fine. She also was glad not to be a felon.

But now she needed him to get out of her life for good. And out of her head.

Ava tried to peek at her notepad. "How's it going?"

"Don't ask."

"You'll get it. You're a great writer."

"I'm a hack."

"Oh, stop. You are not."

Ava grabbed her things, ready to head out the door. The apartment phone rang. The one they kept pretty much exclusively just in case a casting director wanted to track Ava down and didn't have her cell. Which was also why it was a listed number. Every once in a while a student loan officer or telemarketer would try to reach Sabrina on it.

"If that's for me, I'm not here." She waved the notepad in the air as explanation.

Ava nodded as she picked up the phone, taking it into the other room.

Sabrina stared at the fresh, clean page of her notebook. Not that it mattered whether she was disturbed. She couldn't focus.

This wasn't like her. She didn't get writer's block. Writing was the one thing that was hers. The thing she could count on. The place she could lose herself when she had nowhere else to go. And now?

This was all his fault.

Or rather it was her fault for letting him affect her.

Whoever's fault it was, she had a pile of kissing scenes she didn't want to show for it and no ten-minute play. She dropped her head back and groaned.

Ava reappeared. "Okay to interrupt? I've got some news that might cheer you up."

"They moved the showcase to summer?"

"No. *That* was Lacey Silver's assistant. Ms. Silver would

love for you to send over a script of your choosing for her perusal."

"Lacey Silver?"

"Yes! How awesome is that? Did you send a query letter?"

She had not. Lacey Silver was currently the hottest Broadway producer there was. Sabrina would never in a million years have dreamed of approaching her. It was understood that her office dealt only with proven artists— award winners. Or high-profile patrons . . . the societal elite.

People like Noah Prince. Who happened to "know someone" who was a Broadway producer . . .

"I didn't send them anything," she said stiffly.

"Well then, how did they know . . . ?" Ava gasped. "Ooooooh! Oh my God! Do you know what this means?"

"Prince Charming strikes again."

"Well, yeah. Because maybe he *likes* you."

"He doesn't like me. He's got some kind of knight-in-shining-armor complex. He's just trying to do the right thing. It doesn't mean he *likes* me. We knew each other for five minutes. He dates *Victoria Ashby.*"

"Not anymore."

"He dates women *like* Victoria Ashby. And even if he were interested, I'm not."

Ava raised an eyebrow.

"I'm *not.*" There was only one way she was going to get Ava to drop this. She mentally apologized for the white lie she was about to tell. "Honestly, he was kind of a dick."

"Really?"

"Yeah, you know, full of himself, kind of spoiled."

"But he did all those nice things."

She shrugged. "Yeah. He was still full of himself."

"Ugh, that's the worst. Why didn't you say so before?"

She shrugged. "I didn't want to ruin him for you."

Ava wrinkled her nose. "Well, then forget him."

"Exactly."

"Okay, hun, well I'm off to work. Good luck with the wordsmithing. I know you can do it." Ava gave her a hug, then headed out the door, leaving Sabrina alone in the quiet apartment.

Right. Back to work.

Except if she thought she was having trouble getting him out of her mind before, now it was truly hopeless.

Maybe she just shouldn't fight it anymore.

Actually . . .

Maybe she *shouldn't* fight it anymore. If his stupid (gorgeous) face kept wanting to insert itself into her play, who was she to stop it?

Suddenly the ideas were flowing, and Sabrina was scribbling out words as fast as she could to keep up.

This was going to be awesome.

CHAPTER TWENTY-THREE

*J*ust over a week later, Sabrina stood in her robe in front of her closet, trying to choose an outfit. It was the night of the showcase. She should be excited. She always loved watching her work performed—certainly not something she got to do every day. And she was proud of what she'd written. It was a definite departure from her previous work, satirical and over-the-top. Really way out of character for her, but that was the point.

Still, try as she might, her head was still stuck back in that storm. In that car. With that billionaire.

Ava knocked on the door and leaned in.

"Hey, Bree, are we going to walk over together?"

"Sure. I just need to jump in the shower."

"Can I tell you how jazzed I am to do your one-act?" Ava beamed. She was playing the female lead.

"You have to say that, you're my BFF."

"No, for real. Everything you do is great, but this one is

so different. Funny and weird and . . . out there. It's going to be a blast."

She wished she was as enthusiastic as Ava. She was looking forward to it. To seeing her satirical send-up of romance on stage. When she'd been unable to get the events of February 14 out of her head, she'd opted for a cathartic retelling—with artistic license, of course—of those events. But. Well, catharsis was supposed to get the feelings out, right? So they'd go away?

Yeah, not so much. She might have succeeded in distracting herself for a little while, but when she emerged from her writing cocoon? Yep, those feelings were still right where she'd left them. Just below the surface. Refusing to budge.

She, however, was not going to tell Ava that.

"Thanks," she said, looking down. "I'm glad you like it."

Ava turned to look at her more closely. "You're still moping."

"I'm not moping."

"Sabrina."

"I'm fine."

"Are you? You're not sleeping, you've been eating nothing but coffee and ice cream, and no offense, but your room's kind of a mess. I had it chalked up to the intense writing week, but . . . should I be worried?"

"I'm *fine*." She grabbed her towel. "I'll be ready in a few."

She headed out the door before Ava could raise any more objections.

"Okay," Ava called after her. "All right if I at least take out your recycling? Your bin is really full."

That was because it was stuffed with all those sappy

romance scenes she'd written starring thinly veiled versions of her and Noah. And even one or two that just plain actually starred her and Noah, when she'd hoped she might get it out of her system. Yeah, definitely time for those pages to be turned to mulch so that no one could ever, ever see what an idiot she was. "Knock yourself out!"

~

NOAH WAS STILL AT WORK, though it was almost seven, and everyone else had gone home. It was company policy for people to leave work at a reasonable hour. Part of the Prince Resort Hotels philosophy that made them a top-rated employer, in fact. And Noah made sure to enforce it, wanting his staff to have lives. Ironic, since he hadn't thought that important for himself until recently.

And now that he did, well, he didn't have anyone to share it with. So here he was, staying late on a Friday night.

It was clearly not helping. He'd been trying to sort through plans for the new property, hoping to distract himself, but at this point he really wasn't focusing at all. It was time to call it a night.

Not that the solitude of his penthouse was all that appealing. Maybe he'd watch a movie. Or rather put one on and stare at it and try not to think about Sabrina.

He slid on his coat and stepped out of his office to discover Sally still at her desk. Almost certainly because she was keeping an eye on him. She'd always had a protective, maternal streak toward him, but it had been out in force the last couple of weeks. It was touching, but he hated to think of her worrying about him. Surely she had better things to do with her time.

He was about to scold her for staying when the phone rang.

"Noah Prince's office, how may I help you?" She glanced up at him, taking stock of his coat and briefcase. "I'm sorry, miss, I believe he's left for the day."

It couldn't be. He knew Sally would have put her through right away—he had told her to do as much—but he couldn't help himself. "Is it her?"

Sally shook her head. "I'm sorry, sir. It's an Ava Jenkins."

Ava was calling him? "Put her through."

Sally looked surprised. "Of course, Mr. Prince."

He dashed into his office and picked up the receiver. "Ava? Is everything okay? Is Sabrina all right?"

It was the first place his mind went. Why else would she call him?

The woman on the other end of the phone gave a light laugh. "She's fine, don't worry. But that answers that question."

"What question?"

"Whether you like her as much as she likes you."

He'd been pacing in front of his desk, but now he froze. Every cell in his body came to attention. "She said that?"

Another laugh.

"Oh, hell no. She said she can't stand you."

He grinned in spite of himself. That sounded about right.

"But," Ava continued, "what she *wrote*, then buried in her trash can where she thought I wouldn't find it, *that's* a different story."

His mind was racing. Could it be true? Did she have feelings for him after all? Was it not too late? What would he say to her? Would she even listen to him?

"What do I do, Ava?"

"I'm so glad you asked." Mischief laced her voice. "What are you up to right now?"

## CHAPTER TWENTY-FOUR

*S*abrina sat in the front row of the tiny theater. Ava and her scene partner were on stage performing her play. It was just a staged reading—scripts in hand, no costumes. But it was still a treat to see actors breathing life into her words. And getting a piece in front of an audience—even the small smattering of class members' friends and family that had shown up today—was always useful.

It didn't hurt that they seemed to be enjoying her work.

Ava was absolutely nailing the comedy of the script—a crazy, fractured fairy tale, romantic mishmash laid over a structure based loosely on certain events.

Yes, she had borrowed heavily from her experiences in the wilds of Connecticut with Noah Prince. But now the female character was a down-on-her-luck baker-turned-dog-walker-turned-wedding-planner whose mother would not stop trying to fix her up. And Prince Charming was a literal prince (circa 1800 or so) in full regalia (including an oversized sword that kept banging into everything). The heroine had gotten a flat tire, and the prince was insisting on rescuing her, even though she clearly had a better handle on the situation than he did.

"Let me borrow your communication device and I will hail a craftsman to come assist with your carriage."

Ava rolled her eyes. "It's a Toyota, and I'm fine, but thanks."

"Nonsense!" said the actor playing the prince, really getting into the role. He stepped forward, tripped over his sword, and masterfully tumbled to a stop at Ava's feet. "Milady."

Ava just shook her head. The audience roared and clapped.

Sabrina clapped along with them. This kind of comedy was a departure for her, and she was pretty happy with how it had turned out. Well, sort of happy. How was it that she'd made him utterly ridiculous and she was still kind of swooning for him? The guy playing him wasn't even that hot.

"Milady," said the actor again, attempting to scramble to his feet and chase after Ava, who was rounding the chairs that served as the car for the purposes of the reading. "Milady, please, you are not making rescuing you very easy."

The audience erupted in laughter again. The actors held for the reaction, but before they could start up with their lines again, a voice came from the back of the theater.

"That's not exactly how I remember it."

Sabrina froze.

It couldn't be.

ALL EYES TURNED TO NOAH, but there was only one set he was looking for.

He found them staring back at him from the front row, blue and bright, looking equal parts furious and beautiful. It knocked the wind out of him.

Maybe Ava was wrong. Maybe she didn't want him at all. Maybe he shouldn't be here. But it was too late now.

On stage, the actors had stopped. The audience had turned in their seats. Everyone was watching him, waiting to see what he would do next.

"Is this part of the play?" a woman whispered.

"Isn't that Noah Prince?" said someone else.

The actress on stage was watching him carefully. When he looked up at her, she winked. Ava. He gave her the slightest of nods, but somehow Sabrina picked up on it, whirling to throw her friend a death glare. Ava gave her a meaningful look, nodding in his direction.

Sabrina turned back to him. Oh God. Who knew what she would do when she heard what he had to say?

This was a new feeling for him. Uncertainty. Utter terror. Usually he had a pretty good idea of how things were going to go. He liked to be prepared. Do his homework. But there was no homework for this. This was a caution-to-the-wind, seat-of-your-pants kind of move. The stuff of epic romance. Or epic failures.

Here went nothing.

He took several steps toward her.

Sabrina stepped out into the aisle. A camera flashed. The room was stock-still.

"Why are you here?" she whispered as loud as she could (as if that would somehow keep the several dozen people watching them from listening in).

He stepped closer to her, reaching into his pocket. "I have your shoe. You disappeared before I could return it." He held it out to her.

She eyed it skeptically, then arched a brow. "Don't you think that's a little cliché?"

"I do. You can write it out of the stage play version."

THE AUDIENCE—THEIR audience—spoke in excited whispers around them as Sabrina tried to process what was happening.

He came. Here. He was here for her. In front of all these people. People with cell phone cameras and quite possibly the hotlines to the major New York gossip columnists on speed dial, judging by the buzzing energy in the room.

A woman behind him scurried around to get a better angle with her phone, which appeared to be shooting video.

If he wasn't interested, if he didn't care, he was making a hell of a scene for nothing.

But the way he was looking at her, he didn't seem too concerned . . . which left only one possibility: he really wanted to be here. He wanted her.

"What makes you so sure there's going to be a stage play version?" she asked, stepping toward him.

"Why wouldn't there be? It makes a great story, doesn't it? Except for one thing."

"What's that?" she asked as she arrived in front of him. Some wise-guy crew member turned a spotlight on them. She squinted up into Noah's eyes.

"You have to tell me how it ends."

The spotlight operator made an adjustment, and Sabrina could see again. The light glinted off his eyes. Everything around them faded until it was just the two of them as far as she was concerned.

And Sabrina allowed herself, finally, to give in utterly, completely, body and soul, to the romance of the moment. If this was what the universe wanted of her, far be it from her to get in its way.

"It ends like all fairy tales do. With a kiss."

She flung her arms around him as the audience erupted in applause. She was pretty sure she heard Ava whistle, and the woman doing sound for the show played a sweeping, romantic musical cue. But Sabrina hardly noticed any of it as she tangled her hands in Noah's hair and he pulled her tight to him, brushing his lips against hers, first gently, then not so gently. She sank into the kiss and gave herself over to her very own—very real—Valentine's fantasy.

EPILOGUE

*H*e had refused to actually tell her where they were going, though it had been clear since they'd crossed the Connecticut line and turned onto the smaller highway. He signaled his lane change, despite there being not another soul on the road. He was definitely a by-the-book driver. A little tense still, she could tell. But pretty damn good for a guy who had only learned to drive at the age of 29.

She reached over and squeezed his hand. "So, why all the mystery?"

"No mystery," he said, totally unconvincingly. He was almost as terrible an actor as Sabrina was.

It was sweet, though, him bringing her back here for their first Valentine's together. Well, their second, of course. But their first together together. It had been an amazing year. It was hard not to think of how far they'd come, driving up this road again. She hoped he'd thought to check with his parents and make sure they hadn't decided on another romantic getaway to the house. She and the Princes had gotten to know each other over the last year, and she loved them like family, but *that* would be awkward.

She watched the trees roll by, snow blanketing the ground (but, mercifully, not falling from the sky this time). It was dusk, and the fading blue light cast the whole scene in a soft, dreamy haze. Through the trees the amber glow of house lights shone in the distance. It reminded her of someone.

"Oh! Can we go visit Gladys?"

A smile spread across his face. "I'd like that. But first, I need to take care of something."

He eased to a stop at the side of the road and killed the engine. So this was interesting.

"Um . . . what are we doing, Noah?"

He swung around and reached into the backseat of the small car, producing a sweater. His sweater. The one he had lent her during their adventure last year. He handed it to her.

"Just going for a little walk."

"But—"

"Put it on. I don't want you to get cold."

He hopped out of the car, jogging around to her side to open her door, and beamed at her. Whatever was going on, she clearly wasn't going to find out unless she played along.

She pulled on the sweater, then took his hand as he helped her out of the car. Instead of letting her hand go when she stood, he pulled her to him, leaning down to plant one perfect kiss on her lips. He drew back slowly, watching her eyes.

"I still don't—"

Across the street, through the woods, a series of lights blinked on. White twinkle lights, thousands of them, hanging high in the branches, draped between the trees. They were beautiful.

"What is this?" she whispered, releasing Noah's hand to cross the pavement, stepping slowly under the canopy of lights. She could hear his footsteps crunching softly behind her.

There were so many of them, filling the space around them, shining down on them in a spot that had suddenly started to feel very familiar.

And she knew. What this was. What he was doing. She started tearing up. Of course she did. Why didn't men know to warn women when they needed to wear waterproof mascara?

She drew a shaky breath, gazed up at the lights, and said her line. "It's like they're shining just for us."

She turned to find him on one knee, holding out—of course—the world's most perfect diamond ring. "Maybe they are."

His eyes were locked on hers, brimming with love and fear and uncertainty. How could he not know?

"Sabrina, will you—"

"Yes!"

She tackled him to the ground—both of them now covered in snow, and dirt, and random leaves and twigs— and gave him the biggest, best, *messiest* kiss of his life.

Hold on to your hearts, ladies. Billionaire bachelor Noah Prince is off the market! This is not a drill.

The formerly eligible Prince Charming has announced his engagement to his frequent companion of the past year, up-and-coming playwright Sabrina Hopewell. We all used to think Prince was so serious, but his relationship with the soon-to-be Mrs. Prince let us all see his fun side (and for that, Ms. Hopewell, we are eternally grateful and might even forgive you for stealing Noah's heart. Someday.)

From the theater scene to the club scene, we've all been happy we've seen the straightlaced, straight-up hottie loosen up a bit this year. No hard feelings to Mr. Prince's former frequent companion, Ms. Victoria Ashby, who even released her own statement congratulating the happy couple. Now that's class with a capital C!

Mr. Prince's ne'er do well brother, Ryder, was also glad to comment on his brother's recent engagement. "I didn't think he had it in him," said the more notorious Prince heir, "that Sabrina is *hot*."

(Ryder and Victoria have recently inspired a few rumors of their own, and while we'd *love* to get Noah's take on *that*, we'll try to stay classy ourselves and save it for another time.)

As for the wedding plans, no date has been announced yet, and they are *mum* on the proposal, but the ring is to die for.

Ms. Hopewell is a playwright whose rom-com *Happily Never After* is currently set to open off-off-off Broadway next month. We know what you're thinking, but Noah Prince told us personally his girlfriend—we mean fiancée —whoa, that's going to take some getting used to—will *not* let him use his connections to help her career in any way. She wants to do this on her own. You know what, girl? You are just making it impossible for us not to like you!

We wish the prince and his princess many happy years together.

## THANK YOU

Thank you for reading *Driving the Billionaire*. I hope you enjoyed it!

If you have a minute, I'd love for you to leave a quick review.

. . . And then be sure to keep turning pages for a few special treats.

he play had eventually resumed and the evening's program had continued, but Sabrina would have been lying if she said she'd noticed anything that happened on stage after Noah had made his entrance. Sure, they'd already had their big public scene, complete with an utterly swoonworthy kiss, but she'd been dying to get some time alone with him ever since. Which was why she was more than happy to accept his offer to see her home. And conveniently, he'd had a car waiting right out front.

She slid into the back seat, playfully pulling him in after her by his tie, kissing him as she giggled. He somehow managed to close the door without removing his lips from hers.

The driver cleared his throat in the front seat. "Where to, Mr. Prince?"

Noah looked up, dazed, as if he'd forgotten the man was there. "Give us a minute, James."

"Of course, sir." James nodded as the divider rose behind him.

Clever fellow, that James.

Sabrina went to pull Noah back to her. Somehow she'd lost one of those warm, strong arms he'd had wrapped around her, which just wouldn't do. But when she looked, she discovered why. Noah was reaching over to hold a button on the armrest. The divider window finished its ascent, sealing them in cozy silence.

Good, now they could get back to—hang on . . .

"Is that . . . Did you? . . . Can a person *always* control the divider from the backseat?"

Noah looked down sheepishly. He seemed to be suppressing a laugh.

"Noah?"

He nodded. "Pretty much. Mmm-hmm. Yes."

"And you didn't see fit to mention this to me on our little trip? When I was struggling to raise the stupid thing and *not* look like a total idiot?"

"I *was* a bit preoccupied," he said quietly.

Fair enough. "You could have mentioned it later, though."

The corner of his mouth curled up. "And also it was a little adorable."

Sabrina gasped. The nerve of this man! She swatted at him, but he snatched her hand and pulled her close once again.

"Forgive me?" he asked, a whisper away from her lips.

She searched his eyes. As if there were any question.

"Always."

And then she closed the gap.

## CHAPTER ONE

"I'm sorry, Victoria. I know it's short notice."

It was, in fact, a matter of hours. But it wasn't that.

After all, it wasn't that surprising that a man as busy as Davis King would call to cancel their date at the last minute. Especially considering he was on the other side of the country in San Francisco.

She'd known from the outset that cultivating a romantic relationship with a workaholic who lived three thousand miles away wasn't going to be easy. But Davis's commitment to his family's entertainment empire had been one of his biggest appeals.

The steadfast work ethic was something they had in common. And when they had collaborated on a charity project involving one of the King theme parks last year, they had hit it off. Not to mention, Davis ticked nearly all the boxes on Vicky's list. (Yes, she had a list. The best way to get what you want is to be methodical.) Given all that, the distance had seemed like a mere inconvenience. But today not so much. Because today was the Pink Heart Ball, New York's premier Valentine's fundraiser, benefiting women's heart health.

"I'm disappointed, of course, but I understand," she said diplomatically.

"Are you sure? I feel terrible. I know how much the night means to you."

He wasn't wrong. In addition to supporting an important cause and always being an amazing evening, the event drew the elite of the elite. Anyone who wanted to be a power player in the city, whether for profit or, as in her case, for philanthropic purposes, had to be there and at their networking best.

Not to mention, this would be Vicky's first Pink Heart Ball alone. Alone as in unattached, since Noah Prince, her business partner, had ceased to also be her romantic partner. And now, it seemed, alone as in without even a date.

It wasn't that she minded the breakup with Noah. Not anymore anyway. After a year, the wounds were healed, and it was clear to her that they had always been better suited as friends and colleagues. But she was used to having someone at her side at these things. And the media . . . Well, they would notice that she showed up alone. It would be the headline.

Meanwhile, "Prince Charming" (the media's nickname for Noah) wasn't even going to be at the Pink Heart Ball this year. He was off on some mysterious getaway with his girlfriend, which left Vicky to represent the Prince Foundation on her own. No pressure.

She knew she was capable. She didn't *need* a successful businessman on her arm to prove herself. Was it so wrong that she felt more secure if she had one, though? And she was eager to strengthen her relationship with Davis. She wanted a man in her life. Business and society were infinitely easier that way, and truthfully, she was lonely.

Enough. Nothing she could do about the situation now.

"Yes, I'm sure, Davis. Really. I'll see you at the World Media Equality Conference in Madrid next month."

He let out a sigh on the other end of the line. "I had to cancel Madrid. Too much at stake with the new film premier. I need to be on-site in LA. I'm sending a representative, of course, but I won't be there in person."

"Oh. Well, all right. Then at the Children's Literacy Summit in April."

He sucked in air. "Actually, I'll be in Tokyo going over the character design for the new video game that week," he said apologetically.

Vicky shook her head, laughing. She had liked him *because* he was so committed to his work, she reminded herself. "Well, then perhaps we should just have your assistant text my assistant to keep me apprised of your whereabouts on the globe. I can't keep up."

"That's actually not a bad idea!"

"Oh now, Davis, I *was* kidding. I hardly think we need to involve our employees in our relationship." She cringed as soon as the word was out of her mouth. *Was* it a relationship? Did he think of it that way? The last thing she wanted was to push him away by being too presumptuous.

"No, no. Not that. But what if . . . That is, if you don't

think it's *too* much . . . Well, how would you feel about sharing locations?"

Relief washed over her, followed by confusion. It took her a moment. But she thought she saw where he was going.

She cautiously asked, "You mean as in with our phones?"

"Yes, I mean, if you want to. I don't know. Is that silly?" He sounded adorably embarrassed. "I just thought—never mind."

"No! No, I think it's a wonderful idea."

It was sweet really. Him wanting to let her know what he was up to at any given time. The sort of thing you only did with those who were more important to you.

They each tapped the necessary settings into their phones. She looked down at the little map on the screen, which now showed her Davis's location in the King Tower in downtown San Francisco. She smiled to herself. It did make her feel more connected to him somehow.

"I see you," she announced.

"I see you too," he said back, his voice low and gentle in her ear.

And for that moment, it almost felt like she wasn't alone.


CHAPTER TWO

SEVERAL HOURS LATER, Vicky stepped through the entrance of the hotel ballroom and paused to survey the scene. Men in tuxedos, women in evening gowns, classical musicians providing a stirring, romantic soundtrack, champagne, and waltzing couples. Glamour to the hilt.

Vicky, of course, fit right in. She wore her black locks smoothed into elegant waves, and her long, crimson dress draped her lithe figure in lush fabric. Making her look, she knew, every bit like someone out of another time. Like a Golden Age Hollywood starlet walking the red carpet (handy, since she'd just had to walk one on her way in here). It was a trick of her mother's, part of the legacy she'd left her, along with her striking looks. A simple hack: dress like you have all the confidence in the world; the feeling will follow.

And she needed all the confidence she could get tonight.

Of course, her beauty was not in question. If she had to read another glossy magazine article extolling her physical features, she might explode. (She wouldn't, of course. She graciously accepted invitations to be spotlighted on a regular basis, politely slipping in as much as she could about whatever cause the foundation was championing at that moment, using the publicity to its best advantage whenever she could.)

But it didn't exactly make her feel respected as a businesswoman and a force in the charity world when every article spent more space on her eyebrow shape than her latest accomplishment.

Attending this evening's event on her own wasn't helping. Since the breakup with Noah, she may or may not have laid low whenever humanly possible, sending regrets to most of the big events. But she couldn't very well miss the Pink Heart Ball. Especially with her ex-boyfriend/current business partner MIA.

Ugh. Why couldn't Davis have just set aside his amazing work ethic for one evening?

It didn't matter now. She was here. She could do this. She inhaled deeply, poised herself, and let the breath out. Here went nothing.

But just as she began to take a step into the room, she heard raised voices behind her echoing through the hotel lobby.

"Sir, sir! You can't go in there!"

"I can go anywhere I want." Familiar voices. Well, voice. "I'm a *Prince*."

Vicky closed her eyes and counted to—about two and a half as it turned out.

"Sir!" squeaked what could only be the couldn't-be-more-than-twenty-year-old the hotel had foolishly stationed at the door, obviously panicked. There was a flurry of footsteps. "Sir! I'm afraid I'm going to have to ask you and your"—he cleared his throat awkwardly—"party to leave."

Why this? Why today? Did she really want to know who was in the "party"? She did not.

"Does he mean *me*?" gasped an offended-sounding but ridiculously squeaky female voice, just a few feet behind Vicky now. The voice then let out a *harrumph*, followed by what sounded like aggressive snapping of gum.

A low, rumbling laugh followed, even closer to Vicky, which she felt all through her body. It wasn't her fault. Ryder Prince had that effect on most women, and he often used it to its full advantage. It was how he'd managed to become one of the world's most notorious playboys.

She sighed. Unfortunately, he was a notorious playboy she felt a certain amount of responsibility for. The last thing the Princes—her ex's parents who were still her friends as well as her employers—needed was to be embarrassed by their elder son crashing an important society event and making trouble.

"Listen, junior," the man in question was now saying, presumably to the hotel kid, "Maybe your superiors didn't explain this to you too well, but it isn't your job to piss off the guests at these things, so I suggest you—"

Vicky steeled herself and spun around.

"Oh. Well, hello, Vic."

Ryder Prince grinned at her as he removed his muscular arm from the kid's shoulders just in time to keep the poor guy from wetting his pants, as far as she could tell.

"Ryder."

"Who's this?" the gum-cracking ingenue said, clearly unimpressed. She appeared to be dressed for clubbing, in fishnets and a very short dress. As were the other two women hanging on Ryder, one in a nearly see-through top, another in not so much a top as what appeared to be a leather bra.

Ryder, though, was in a tux. Which was, let's say, momentarily distracting. Because troublemaker or not, the man looked awfully good in a tux.

He shook off his groupies and took a step toward her, offering her a lopsided smile.

"How's it hanging, Vic?"

That was the thing about Ryder. There was no denying

his charm, but (mercifully), he usually managed to ruin it once he opened his mouth.

"It's *hanging* just fine, Ryder. But what are you doing here? Formal charity events aren't really your thing."

"I'm expanding my horizons."

"There's a line not to be crossed, Ryder. I know you know this. Crashing the Pink Heart Ball is too much. Be reasonable."

He arched a dark brow. "Come now, princess, we both know Ryder Prince is never reasonable."

"Are we going in or what, Ryde?" whined see-through-shirt woman. "I'm thirsty. You said there'd be champagne."

The pubescent hotel kid cleared his throat again. "I'm sorry, but without an invitation—"

"I have an invitation."

"You do?" Vicky said before she could stop herself.

Ryder reached into his jacket pocket and produced one of the official engraved invitation cards. He grinned at her unconcealed confusion. "The folks got me on the list. Must be hoping for a miraculous transformation."

He had to be telling the truth. Not only did she not believe Ryder would outright lie, but the guest list to the event was exclusive—invitations were not easy to come by. Someone had to have added him to the list. And no one would have been so foolish as to invite the black sheep of the Prince family without their blessing. Cheryl and Warren must have arranged this themselves.

She wondered what they could have been thinking. But even as she thought this, she realized it had to have been Cheryl and her eternal optimism winning out again. Optimism that definitely would not have imagined Ryder parading around the ball with a mini harem.

"So, what's it gonna be, Vic? You going to call security and make a scene here?" He waggled his eyebrows at her. The devil.

She took a step closer. She wasn't about to be intimidated by the likes of him. "Fine. But you come in alone."

Gum Girl gasped in outrage. "Ryde, tell this slut to get lost."

Ryder didn't take his eyes off Vicky. He stayed silent for a minute. Thinking, or maybe just drawing the moment out to try to get to her.

"I don't travel alone," he said finally.

"Oh, you won't be alone. You'll be with me," she clarified. It wasn't like she was dying to have to chaperone an errant bad boy all night, but he was far less likely to cause trouble in there with her than without her, and trying to get him to leave when he didn't want to would just cause a scene and all the accompanying bad publicity. Cheryl and Warren, not to mention Prince Resort Hotels and the Prince Foundation, definitely did not need that.

"With you?" Ryder raised a brow.

She nodded.

He looked her up and down, considering. She ignored the slight flutter in the stomach this induced.

"Fine," he said.

"What?" growled Leather Bra.

"Sorry, ladies, I'm afraid the invitation is, officially, just for one. I'm going to have to bid you farewell."

"Tch. We don't need this. Come on, girls." See-Through

Shirt led the others away, their stilettos clicking in unison on the floor as they departed.

Ryder turned to the hotel kid, slipping him a hundred-dollar bill. "Put them in a cab to wherever they want to go, would ya?" He slipped him another fifty. "That's for you."

"R-right away, sir," stammered the kid. He ran off after the women.

Ryder pinned his eyes on Victoria. He chuckled. "'Sir.' Poor slob has no idea."

Vicky just looked him up and down before shaking her head. "Come on, then. And you'd better behave yourself."

He hooked his elbow, holding it out for her to take.

"I always behave myself." He flashed her a wicked grin. "Of course, it might depend on your definition of behaving."

"Like a *gentleman*, Ryder." She took his arm. "I want you to behave like a gentleman."

"Oh. Well, you should have said."

Vicky groaned as she let him lead her into the ballroom. What had she gotten herself into?

Get Chaperoning the Billionaire on Amazon

# ABOUT THE AUTHOR

Laurie Baxter has degrees in both puppetry and screen-writing because let's face it, majoring in English would have been no more useful and way less fun. She loves chocolate, ice cream, chocolate ice cream, dogs, New York City, old movies, modern architecture, all kinds of theater, and music from before she was born. Her eighth grade English teacher told her to become a writer, so she did.

lauriebaxter.com

- amazon.com/author/lauriebaxter
- bookbub.com/profile/laurie-baxter
- facebook.com/LaurieBaxterAuthor
- goodreads.com/LBaxWrites
- instagram.com/lbaxwrites

Made in the USA
Columbia, SC
03 June 2024